CW00621806

Right: route planning by the
château at Josselin, France

CONTENTS

Published by RAC Publishing, RAC House, PO Box 100, South Croydon, Surrey, CR2 6XW

© RAC Motoring Services Limited 1996

ISBN 0 86211 364 4 (Members edition)

ISBN 0 86211 374 1 (Trade edition)

Printed and bound by: Grafo, S.A., Bilbao, Spain

Escape

At the RAC we can release you from
the worries of motoring

But did you know that we can also
give you invaluable peace of mind
when you go on holiday,

Or arrange your hotel bookings,

Or even organise your entire
holiday, all over the phone?

RAC Travel Insurance   0800 550 055

RAC Hotel Reservations   0345 056 042

RAC Holiday Reservations   0161 480 4810

Call us

PREPARING FOR THE JOURNEY

DOCUMENTS

Before a journey, allow plenty of time to arrange for the preparation of all necessary documents – passports, visas, driving licences, insurances and vaccinations. The RAC will give advice on what documents are required for which countries; remember to ask about countries visited in transit as well as your destination country. The following information applies only to British Subjects holding, or entitled to, a Foreign Office passport bearing the inscription "United Kingdom of Great Britain and Northern Ireland".

Non-British citizens travelling in Europe should apply to their Embassy, Consulate or High Commission for information if in doubt.

Passports

Although continental European countries have abandoned routine passport checks at land frontiers, visitors are still expected to be able to provide proof of identity by way of a valid passport or identity card while in their country. It is a legal obligation in certain countries to carry such a document at all times. In addition, carrying a passport will help airline and ferry companies with passenger checks; obtaining assistance from British consular posts; hotel registration; banking services; and when returning to UK at immigration controls.

Each person in the party must hold, or be named on, a current passport valid for the countries of visit. Children under 16 may be included on the parents' passport, but if they are likely to travel independently on overseas school educational trips, a separate passport should be held, The issue of 'family passports' including the particulars of wife/husband has been discontinued, however existing documents issued may continue to be used until expiry.

A UK passport of 32 pages costs £18 and 48 pages costs £27. Both are valid for 10 years. Two photographs of not more than 45mm by 35mm (1.77in x 1.38in) are required, one of which should be signed on the reverse by a doctor, lawyer, MP or person of similar standing who has known the applicant for more than two years. The passport application form should also be countersigned by the same person.

Passport application forms are available from main post offices. Completed forms, the fee, photographs and appropriate enclosures should be returned to a regional Passport Office, determined by your home address, for processing. The addresses of the Passport Offices are given on the application form. Passport Office hours of business are Mon-Fri 0900 – 1630hrs, except the London office (open to personal callers only) which closes at 1600hrs. Applications should be sent at least one month before the passport is needed. The peak period for passport applications is Jan-July so it is advisable to apply in the autumn if a new passport is required for the following year.

Passport Agency information line ☎ 0990 210410.

Visas

At the time of going to press, British nationals need a visa for Bulgaria, the CIS, Romania and Turkey. Visa regulations are subject to change however, and it is advisable to contact the Consulate of the appropriate country well in advance of your departure date. Non-UK passport holders should check the visa requirements with the appropriate Embassy/Consulate of the countries to be visited.

Work Permits

Should the stay abroad exceed three months, or if repeated visits are made, or if employment is being sought (even on a temporary basis), a work permit may be required.

Driving Licences

A valid, full driving licence should be carried by all motorists in Europe. Most European countries recognise a UK driving licence, although reference should be made to the appropriate country in the Europe by Country section of this guide.

An International Driving Permit (IDP) is normally required in those countries where a UK licence is not recognised. Valid for one year, this is an internationally recognised document available for drivers holding a valid, full licence and aged 18 or over. The IDP currently costs £4.00 and application forms are available from RAC Travel Services, ☎ 0800 55 00 55. A passport-size photograph is required, in addition to a current driving licence. If a locally registered vehicle is hired in the CIS, Algeria or Morocco, an IDP is required.

In Europe people under 18 are not normally permitted to drive. (Warning:European car hire companies may restrict drivers under 21 or even under 25.) Your driving licence should be carried with you as it must be produced at once, on demand; there is no discretionary period as in the UK.

Holders of 'green' style licences may exchange these licences for an EC format 'pink/green' licence on completion of the D1 application form available from main post offices. A fee of £6.00 should accompany the application to DVLA, Swansea.

Holders of non-UK licences requiring an IDP, must apply to the relevant licensing authority or motoring organisation in the country in which the licence was issued.

Motor Insurance

INTERNATIONAL MOTOR INSURANCE CERTIFICATE (GREEN CARD)

Motor vehicle insurance for minimum Third Party risks is compulsory in Europe. This is provided by most UK and Eire policies covering all EU countries and certain other European countries. Unless your insurer is notified that you are travelling in Europe, your Comprehensive Insurance may be automatically reduced to Third Party Cover. The Green Card provides additional evidence that third party cover is held but it is not a legal requirement. Contact your insurers for advice.

A Green Card is compulsory in Andorra, Bulgaria, Poland and Romania. A Green Card is strongly recommended for travel in Spain, Portugal, Italy and Greece. Your Green Card should be valid for both the European and Asian sectors when travelling in Turkey. When taking a caravan abroad, you should check with

your insurance company that your policy covers towing a caravan in Europe as you may have to pay an extra premium.

A bail bond is strongly recommended for Spain and this is available from your motor insurers, or by taking out the RAC's European Motoring Assistance which includes £1,500 bail bond cover.

Vehicle Registration Document

A vehicle registration document must be carried when driving a UK-registered vehicle abroad. If the document is in the process of being replaced at the time of travelling, you can apply for a free Certificate of Registration (V379) at your local Vehicle Registration Office*. This is internationally recognised in lieu of the registration document and should be carried with you. Should the vehicle not be registered in your name, eg a company car, written authority for you to use it should be obtained from its owner. A special form of authority should be used in this case when travelling in Portugal and this can be obtained from the RAC.

Taking a hired or leased vehicle abroad requires a Vehicle on Hire/Lease Certificate (VE 103) as the vehicle registration document is held by the leasing company and this can be obtained from RAC Travel Information on ☎ 0345 333 222.

A closure plan of Vehicle Registration Offices has commenced. For further advice contact RAC Travel Information ☎ 0345 333 222.

Loss of Documents

Should any of the above documents be lost or stolen, immediately notify the nearest police station; inform the RAC and the National Club of the country concerned. Foreign Customs can enforce payment of duty in lieu of evidence of export if your vehicle is stolen or destroyed by fire. Indemnity covering this is provided for under the RAC European Motoring Assistance providing that reasonable security measures have been taken.

MEDICAL REQUIREMENTS

A useful booklet "Health Advice for Travellers"(ref.T5) is available from post offices and by telephoning the Health Literature Line ☎ 0800 55 57 77 any time, free of charge. Free or reduced cost emergency treatment is available in the European Economic Area (EEA) countries on production of form E111 found in the

above booklet which must be counter-signed by the post office before use. However, travellers should note that cover under this scheme is **minimal** and it is strongly recommended to arrange additional travel insurance such as RAC European Personal Travel Insurance. For details call ☎ 0800 55 00 55.

ESSENTIAL ACCESSORIES

RAC Travel Centres can supply most of the accessories which are useful or helpful when travelling in Europe.

Fire extinguishers

A fire extinguisher is an essential accessory for all vehicles travelling in the CIS, Estonia, Greece, Lithuania, or Turkey. It is strongly recommended that a fire extinguisher is carried at all times.

First Aid Kit

A First Aid kit must be carried on all vehicles travelling in Austria, Bulgaria, the CIS, Croatia, Czech Republic, Estonia, Greece, Lithuania, Slovakia, Slovenia and Turkey, but is advisable in all countries at all times.

GB Plate

A distinctive nationality plate must be displayed near the rear number plate as a legal requirement in all countries. It must have black letters on a white background and conform to a certain regulatory size as do those issued by the RAC.

Headlamps

Headlamp beams should be adjusted before driving on the right. A headlamp conversion kit makes this an easy task as it contains specially shaped adhesive black plastic, which alters the direction of the beam when stuck to the glass. Don't forget to remove the beam converters on returning to the UK.

Carry spare bulbs of the correct wattage for your lights as they may be difficult to obtain abroad. In Spain and certain other countries it is compulsory to carry a spare set of bulbs.

Snow Chains

Snow chains are a legal requirement during the winter when travelling in alpine countries. They are available from the RAC for purchase or hire and cover most makes of car. Further details from RAC Travel Services ☎ 0800 55 00 55 or they can be collected from the RAC Travel Centres in Dover and Portsmouth.

Warning Triangles

You must carry a warning triangle in Austria, Belgium, Bulgaria, the CIS, Czech Republic, Denmark, Germany, Greece, Hungary, Italy, Lithuania, Luxembourg, Netherlands, Poland, Portugal, Romania, Slovakia, Slovenia and Switzerland. It is recommended to carry one if visiting Ireland, Finland, France, Norway or Sweden. Two are necessary if travelling through Cyprus or Turkey, and Spain (if the vehicle has 9 or more seats or weighs over 3,500kg). Two are required if towing a trailer in Croatia.

Where to Position the Warning Triangle

Warning triangles must be placed on the road at the rear of a vehicle (not a motorcycle) which has broken down on an open road at night, in poor visibility during the day, or on a bend in the road or on a hill. Different countries have different regulations as to how far away from the car the warning triangle should be placed if you need to use it. The specific country requirements can be found on the casing of the RAC Warning Triangle (and on other leading brands).

Tachograph

A tachograph is an essential fitment to all UK-registered vehicles travelling in the EU, which are constructed and equipped to carry ten or more people including the driver. Please refer to your local Department of Transport Traffic Area Office for further information.

PREPARING YOUR CAR

Even well-maintained cars can break down without any warning, but some simple preventive maintenance before you contemplate a long journey can minimise the chances of an unexpected road-side stop.
The main causes of breakdowns are the ignition/electrical system closely followed by the fuel and cooling systems. Preventive maintenance and inspection prior to your journey is quite a simple task and can help avoid the inconvenience and worry associated with a breakdown. Mechanical faults however are another matter, and when a major one occurs – either in the engine, gearbox or axle – a road-side repair is usually not practicable.

BATTERY

The main problems with the battery are usually associated with the two electrical connections to the battery terminals. When corrosion occurs the green or white powder fungus growing on the terminal can prevent power getting from the battery to the starter motor. Even though the connections may appear clean on the exterior, it is advisable to remove the terminal connector* and clean the contact surfaces with a wire brush or emery paper. In order to prevent recurrence of corrosion, apply a smear of petroleum jelly to the connections before they are re-made and again afterwards to cover all outermost surfaces of the connector and battery terminal.
Another common cause for the starter motor not working, apart from the obvious flat battery, is the battery earth lead connection not making proper contact with the body or chassis of the vehicle. If this is the problem, remove the connector and clean as with the main battery terminals.
Check both battery cables and any earth straps for breakage or fraying (this usually occurs at the terminal ends) and replace if necessary. Finally, check the level of the battery electrolyte – that is the fluid inside the battery – which should be just above the battery plates. If the battery plates are exposed, top up using distilled water. Some batteries are sealed for life and topping up is not possible.
*Do remember radio and alarm codes may be lost.

Safety tips

Never smoke whilst working in the vicinity of the battery as it could be giving off an explosive gas. Also, when disconnecting or reconnecting the live battery terminal, be very careful not to allow the spanner to contact any metalwork of the car. This could give you a bad burn or the resulting spark could cause a battery to explode.
To be on the safe side, always remove the battery earth cable first – that is the one connected to the bodywork, chassis or engine – and reconnect it last.

IGNITION SYSTEM

Before attempting to carry out any checks or adjustments on any part of the ignition system, you must ensure that the ignition is switched off.

Contact points*

Remove the distributor cap and this will expose the contact points. The contact points are the most common cause of breakdown in the ignition system. If the contact point faces appear badly pitted or burnt then they will require replacing or cleaning.
The contact point gap is also critical, this can close up after a period of time. Contact point gaps vary from one model to another so consult your vehicle handbook. To check and adjust the contact point gap, it is necessary to rotate the engine until one of the lobes on the distributor cam has pushed the moving arm of the contact points to its fullest open position. Using a feeler gauge, make any adjustment to the gap by slackening the contact breaker retaining screw or screws and move the position of the contact points relative to the distributor base plate. This can usually be best achieved by placing a screwdriver between the adjustment notches and turning. Adjust the contact point gap until the feeler gauge will just fit between the contact points. Lock the adjusting screw and re-check the gap as sometimes the setting can alter when the retaining screw is tightened.
*Not electronic ignition systems

Distributor cap

The distributor cap is another potential problem area. Carry out the following simple checks:
(1)   Check the H.T. leads are secure in the cap.
(2)   Make sure the distributor cap is free from any oil residue, dirt or moisture both inside and outside.
(3)   Examine the rotor arm and distributor cap very closely both inside and outside for any hairline cracks or tracking caused by the H. T. current.
(4)   Whilst the distributor cap is removed, check the centre connector. This should protrude far enough to contact the rotor arm when the cap is replaced. If the

carbon brush is badly worn then a replacement cap will be needed.

H.T. leads

The H.T. leads are the thick cables coming out of the distributor cap. Any breakdown either in the conductive centre, the insulation or at the connections will cause faulty operation of the ignition system. First, wipe the outer insulation material clean and examine for cracking or deterioration. Check the connectors at both ends for security and cleanliness.

Remember that the H.T. leads to the spark plugs must be fitted in the correct positions; if the leads become mixed up, the car will not start. It is a good idea to number the leads to assist you in correct re-installation. Alternatively, only remove one H.T. lead at a time. Modern vehicles are fitted with carbon core type leads which can break down internally. This type of lead can be properly tested only by an auto electrician.

Coil connections

The coil is the source of power for the ignition system and it is vital that the connections for the two low-tension wires either side of the main H.T. lead are both secure and clean. Also, check the main H.T. lead to ensure this is secure. Examine the plastic top of the coil for any hairline cracks or tracking caused by the H.T. current short-circuiting and replace if need be. Finally ensure the coil top is clean of grease, dirt or damp.

FUEL SYSTEM

It is far more difficult to anticipate a breakdown in the fuel system although some simple checks can be carried out to minimise the risk.

(1)   Examine any rubber fuel pipes for age cracking, softening, leakage, and make sure they are secure at the connections.

(2)   Most vehicle fuel systems will incorporate a fuel filter or dirt trap to prevent any debris being transmitted through the fuel lines to the carburettor. Ensure that the periodic checks detailed in the vehicle handbook are carried out – usually either cleaning or replacement.

(3)   Check around the carburettor gasket joints, jet assemblies, and feed pipes for any evidence of fuel leakage. Rectification may require the services of a specialist.

(4)   The efficiency of the engine will greatly depend upon the correct mixture setting for the carburettor. With modern carburettors, this can be checked and reset only by a properly equipped workshop. Excessive exhaust emissions now constitute a legal offence.

COOLING SYSTEM

The efficiency of the engine cooling system is vital when contemplating a continental touring holiday as the climatic conditions and terrain may impose greater strains upon it.

Check the radiator to ensure it is free from external blockage or restrictions. Remove any debris such as leaves, paper or accumulated dirt. Inspect all the rubber coolant hoses for signs of age cracking, bulges (particularly adjacent to the securing clips) and check tightness of hose clips, although avoid overtightening as this will cut into the hose material.

When topping up the cooling system, it is advisable to do so with the recommended anti-freeze solution as anti-freeze contains a corrosion inhibitor to minimise corrosion build-up.

Check the fan belt for fraying, general deterioration or excessive glazing on the V-shape drive surfaces which may promote slip. If there is more than half an inch of free play on the belt's longest run, then some adjustment is required.

If the fan belt has not been replaced during the preceding 12 months then it is a good idea to replace it to avoid any possible inconvenience should it fail. Keep the old fan belt in the boot as a 'get you home' spare.

If your fan belt does break then this will be signalled by the generator/ignition warning light lighting up and an increased reading on the water temperature gauge if one is fitted. The car should be stopped immediately and the belt replaced, in order to minimise damage to the engine. On many diesel engines the brake servo pump is driven by the alternator drive belt and the brakes will lose efficiency.

Finally, do not forget other parts of the vehicle that can break down and cause you considerable inconvenience. Tyres should be checked for condition, tread depth and pressure (see page 10 for notes on the care and use of tyres). Check the exhaust system for condition and security. Last, but certainly not least, check the braking system. If you do not feel competent to do so, call in the experts.

Firestone

CONTROL WHERE YOU NEED IT.

TYRES

PRESSURE

Tyre pressures should be checked weekly, using a reliable gauge, and corrected as necessary. Pressure tests and correction of pressure should be made with the tyres cold and not after a period of running. It may be necessary to increase pressures because of loading or high speeds, particularly in hot countries (refer to the vehicle handbook). Both car and tyre manufacturers provide details of correct pressures for various types of driving conditions. Under-inflation is a frequent cause of tyre failure.

TREAD DEPTH

By law, you must maintain a tread pattern of at least 1.6mm in one continuous band across three-quarters of the tread and around the entire circumference of each tyre. It is advisable to ensure that your spare tyre also complies with this regulation.

ALIGNMENT

Wheel alignment should be checked when abnormal front tyre wear is noted, and after even a minor front-end collision.

SHOCK ABSORBERS

Worn shock absorbers can affect the stability of a car and the life of the tyres. Shock absorbers should be checked visually for oil leaks, and by bouncing the appropriate corner of the car, and replaced when necessary.

WHEEL BALANCE

Wheels should be balanced whenever a tyre is changed or when vibration or wobble becomes apparent.

TYRE DAMAGE

Tyres can be damaged easily by nails, sharp stones, kerbs etc. Avoid brushing against kerbs – this can damage the sidewalls. If you have to drive up a kerb, do so slowly and at as near a right angle as possible to minimise any damage. Inspect tyres regularly; remove any stones or nails lodged in the tread.
It is illegal to drive on a tyre which has a break in its fabric, or a cut over 1 inch long and deep enough to reach the body cords.

TYRE LIFE

Maximum tyre life is largely in the driver's hands, although chassis design and maintenance also play a part. Prolonging tyre life usually means that the performance of the car cannot be exploited to its full extent; thus the driver can choose between obtaining maximum performance from the car or maximum life from the tyres.
Tyre life can be prolonged by: taking corners easily; avoiding high average speeds, especially on rough surfaces; avoiding rapid acceleration and/or violent braking; keeping brakes properly adjusted; avoiding damage by oil, grease, petrol, paraffin etc; maintaining correct pressures.

USEFUL INFORMATION

Boats

It is a good idea to obtain a Certificate of Registration when temporarily importing a boat into Europe. The Small Ships Register, operated by DVLA, covers ships below 24 metres in length. Records include name, owner's details, description of the vessel, and details of make or class. The cost is £10 for a 5-year registration. Details may be obtained from: Small Ships Register, DVLA, Swansea, SA99 1BX, ☎ 01792 783355.

If you are considering taking a boat to the Continent it is advisable to contact the Royal Yachting Association, RYA House, Romsey Road, Eastleigh, Hants S05 4YA, ☎ 01703 629962, for information on documentation and regulations.

Car telephones/CB radios

The use of car telephones and CB radios is restricted in most European countries; contact the RAC or your supplier for further guidance.

Foreign currency

There is no limit on the amount of sterling or foreign currency that may be taken out of the country. It is obviously safer to carry the bulk of your money in travellers' cheques, but it is advisable to have a small amount of cash in the currency of the first country you will be visiting, especially if you are staying there overnight or travelling over a weekend. Major credit cards are widely accepted throughout Europe, and Eurocheques and Eurocheque cards provide a valuable facility for payment and cash withdrawal.

Large sums of currency should be declared to Customs when entering any country - including Britain.

Phrase books

It can be very useful to have a phrase book when travelling on the Continent. Knowledge of the particular language is not necessary as most contain a guide to pronunciation and you can always point to a phrase in the book. You should expect it to cover all the situations you are likely to find yourself in, e.g. at Customs posts, shopping, using public transport.

NATIONAL TOURIST OFFICES

As a number of tourist offices now request a fee to cover postage, it is advisable to enclose a minimum of £1 with written enquiries.

ANDORRA

Andorran Delegation,
63 Westover Road, London SW18 2RF.
☎ 0181-874 4806

AUSTRIA

Austrian National Tourist Office,
30 St George Street, London W1R 0AL.
☎ 0171-629 0461

BELGIUM

Belgian National Tourist Office,
29 Princes Street, London, W1R 7RG.
☎ 0891-887799*

BULGARIA

No official tourist office in UK. All enquiries to:
Balkan Holidays, 19 Conduit Street, London W1R 9TD.
☎ 0171-543 5566 (Customer Services)

CIS

Intourist Travel Ltd, Intourist House,
219 Marsh Wall, London E14 9PD.
☎ 0171-538 5965

CROATIA

Croatian National Tourism Office, 2 The Lanchesters,
162-164 Fulham Palace Road, London W6 9ER.
☎ 0181-563 7979

CYPRUS

Cyprus Tourism Organisation,
213 Regent Street, London W1R 8DA.
☎ 0171-734 9822

CZECH REPUBLIC
Czech Centre,
95 Great Portland Street, London W1N 5RA.
☎ 0891 171266*

DENMARK
Danish Tourist Board, 55 Sloane Street,
London SW1X 9SY. ☎ 0171-259 5959

FINLAND
Finnish Tourist Board,
30-35 Pall Mall, London SW1Y 5LP. ☎ 0171-839 4048

FRANCE
Maison de la France (French Tourist Office),
178 Piccadilly, London W1V 0AL. ☎ 0891-244123*

GERMANY
German National Tourist Office, Nightingale House,
65 Curzon Street, London W1Y 8NE. ☎ 0891-600100*

GIBRALTAR
Gibraltar Information Bureau, Arundel Great Court, 179
The Strand, London WC2R 1EH. ☎ 0171-836 0777

GREECE
National Tourist Organisation of Greece, 4 Conduit
Street, London W1R 0DJ. ☎ 0171-734 5997

HUNGARY
Hungarian National Tourist Board,
PO Box 4336, London SW18 4XE. ☎ 0891-171200*

ITALY
Italian State Tourist Office,
1 Princes Street, London W1R 8AY. ☎ 0891 600280*

LUXEMBOURG
Luxembourg Tourist Office, 122 Regent Street, London
W1R 5FE. ☎ 0171-434 2800

MONACO
Monaco Government Tourist and Convention Office,
3-18 Chelsea Garden Market, Chelsea Harbour,
London SW10 0XE. ☎ 0171-352 9962

NETHERLANDS
Netherlands Board of Tourism,
18 Buckingham Gate, London SW1E 6LB.
☎ 0891-717777*
Postal address: PO Box 523, London SW1E 6NT

NORWAY
Norwegian National Tourist Office, Charles House, 5-11
Lower Regent Street, London SW1Y 4LR.
☎ 0171-839 6255

POLAND
Poland National Tourist Office, 1st Floor, Remo House,
310-312 Regent Street, London W1R 5AJ.
☎ 0171-580 8811

PORTUGAL
Portuguese National Tourist Office,
22-25a Sackville Street, London W1X 2LY.
☎ 0171-494 1441

REPUBLIC OF IRELAND
Irish Tourist Board, 150 New Bond Street,
London W1Y 0AQ. ☎ 0171-493 3201

ROMANIA
Romanian National Tourist Office,
83a Marylebone High Street, London W1M 3DE.
☎ 0171-224 3692

SLOVAKIA
No official tourist office in UK. Limited tourist material
available by sending SAE to: Embassy of Slovakia,
25 Kensington Palace Gardens, London W8 4QY.
☎ 0171-243 0803

SLOVENIA
Slovenian Tourist Office, 2 Canfield Place, London
NW6 3BT. ☎ 0171-372 3767

SPAIN
Spanish National Tourist Office, 57-58 St James's Street,
London SW1A 1LD. ☎ 0891-669920*

SWEDEN
Swedish Travel and Tourism Council,
11 Montagu Place, London W1H 2AL. ☎ 0171 724 5868

SWITZERLAND
Switzerland Tourism, Swiss Centre,
Swiss Court, London W1V 8EE. ☎ 0171-734 1921

TURKEY
Turkish Tourist Office, 1st Floor, 170 Piccadilly,
London W1V 9DD. ☎ 0171-629 7771

*(calls cost 45p per minute cheap rate, 50p per minute
at all other times).*

BRITISH DIPLOMATIC ADDRESSES

ALBANIA
(see Italy, Roma)

ANDORRA
(see Spain, Barcelona)

AUSTRIA
1030 Wien (Vienna)
EMBASSY
Jaurèsgasse 12 ☎ (01) 7131575/9
CONSULATE
Jaurèsgasse 10 ☎ (01) 7146117/18

6923 Bregenz
CONSULATE (HON)
Bundesstrasse 110
☎ (05574) 78586

8010 Graz
CONSULATE (HON)
Schmiedgasse 8-12
☎ (0316) 826105

6021 Innsbruck
CONSULATE (HON)
Matthias-Schmid Strasse 12
☎ (05222) 588320

5020 Salzburg
CONSULATE (HON)
Alter Markt 4 ☎ (662) 848133

BALTIC STATES
ESTONIA
Tallinn EE 0100
EMBASSY
Kentmanni 20
☎ (3726) 313353/461/462

LATVIA
Riga LV 1340
EMBASSY
Elizabetes Iela (3rd floor)
☎ (371) 320737 or 325592

LITHUANIA
2055 Vilnius
EMBASSY
Antakalnio 2
☎ (370) 2222070

BELGIUM
1040 Bruxelles
EMBASSY
Rue d'Arlon 85
☎ (02) 2876211

2000 Antwerpen
CONSULATE-GENERAL (HON)
Korte Klarenstraat 7
☎ (03) 2315719/2326940

4000 Liège
CONSULATE (HON)
rue Beeckman 45 ☎ (041) 235832

BULGARIA
Sofiya 1000
EMBASSY
Boulevard Vassil Levski 65-67
☎ (02) 885361/2, 885325

CIS
RUSSIA
Moskva (Moscow) 72
EMBASSY/CONSULATE
Sofiiskaya, Naberezhnaya 14
☎ (095) 956 7200
Consular/visa section: 230 6333

St Petersburg
CONSULATE-GENERAL
Pl. Proletarskoy Diktatury 5
☎ (0812) 119 6036

UKRAINE
252021 Kiev
EMBASSY/CONSULATE
Kiev Desyatinna 9
☎ (7) 228 0504/229 1287

CROATIA
50000 Dubrovnik
CONSULATE (HON)
Atlas, Pile 1
☎ (050) 27333

58000 Split
CONSULATE (HON)
Titova Obala 10/III
☎ (058) 41464

41000 Zagreb
EMBASSY
Ilica 12/II, PO Box 454
☎ (041) 334245, 339147

CYPRUS
Nicosia
HIGH COMMISSION
Alexander Pallis Street,
PO Box 1978 ☎ (2) 473131/7

CZECH REPUBLIC
12550 Praha (Prague)
EMBASSY
Thunovská 14
☎ (02) 24510439, 24510443

DENMARK
2100 København
(Copenhagen)
EMBASSY
36-38-40 Kastelsvej
☎ 35 26 46 00

6200 Åbenrå
CONSULATE (HON)
Kilen 29 ☎ 74 62 77 00

9200 Ålborg
CONSULATE (HON)
Stationsmestervej 85
☎ 98 18 16 00

8100 Århus
CONSULATE (HON)
Havnegade 8 ☎ 86 12 88 88

6700 Esbjerg
CONSULATE (HON)
Kanalen 1 ☎ 75 13 05 11

7000 Fredericia
CONSULATE (HON)
Vesthavnen, PO Box 235
☎ 75 92 20 00

7400 Herning
CONSULATE (HON)
Orebygaardvej 3-7
☎ 97 26 88 01

5000 Odense
CONSULATE (HON)
Albanitorv 4 ☎ 66 14 47 14

3700 Rønne, Bornholm
CONSULATE (HON)
Fiskerivej 1 ☎ 53 95 21 11

FINLAND
00140 Helsinki
EMBASSY
Itainen Puistotie 17
☎ (90) 661293

40101 Jyväskylä
CONSULATE (HON)
Valmet Paper Machinery Inc.,
PO Box 587
☎ (941) 295211

48100 Kotka
CONSULATE (HON)
Port Authority of Kotka,
Laivurinkatu 7 ☎ (952) 2820291

70100 Kuopio
CONSULATE (HON)
Chamber of Commerce,
Kasarmikatu 2
☎ (971) 2820291

90101 Oulu
CONSULATE (HON)
Rautaruukki Oy,
Kiilakiventie 1, PO Box 217
☎ (981)327711

28101 Pori
CONSULATE (HON)
Repola Oy, Antinkatu 2,
PO Box 51 ☎ (939) 823007

33101 Tampere
CONSULATE (HON)
Oy Finlayson AB, PL 407
☎ (931) 249 4111

20101 Turku
CONSULATE (HON)
Turun Kauppakamari,
Puolalankatu 1
☎ (921) 501440

65100 Vaasa
CONSULATE (HON)
Royal Waasa Sokos Hotel,
Hovioikeudenpuistikko 18
☎ (961) 278111

FRANCE
(*Telephone numbers
changed 18/10/96 see page 92)

Paris
EMBASSY
35 rue du Faubourg St Honoré,
Cedex 08, 75383 Paris
☎ (1) 42 66 91 42

64200 Biarritz
CONSULATE (HON)
"Askenian", 7 blvd Tauzin
☎ (5) 59 24 21 40

33073 Bordeaux
CONSULATE-GENERAL
353 blvd du Président Wilson
☎ (5) 56 42 34 13

62200 Boulogne-sur-Mer
CONSULATE (HON)
Cabinet Barron & Brun "La Carte"
88 - 100 Route de Paris
Saint Martin Boulogne
☎ (3) 21 87 16 80

62100 Calais
CONSULATE (HON)
c/o P & O European Ferries,
41 place d'Armes
☎ (3) 21 96 33 76

50104 Cherbourg
CONSULATE (HON)
c/o P & O European Ferries,
Gare Maritime Sud
☎ (2) 33 44 20 13

59383 Dunkerque
CONSULATE (HON)
c/o L Dewulf, Cailleret & Fils,
11 rue des Arbres, BP 1502
☎ (3) 28 66 11 98

76600 Le Havre
CONSULATE (HON)
c/o Lloyds Register of Shipping,
124 blvd de Strasbourg
☎ (2) 35 42 42 15/27 47

59800 Lille
CONSULATE-GENERAL
11 Square Dutilleul
☎ (3) 20 57 87 90

69002 Lyon
CONSULATE-GENERAL
24 rue Childebert
☎ (4) 78 37 59 67 (4 lines)

13006 Marseille
CONSULATE-GENERAL
24 av du Prado
☎ (4) 91 53 43 32
(also deals with MONACO)

44220 Nantes
CONSULATE (HON)
L'Aumarière, Couëron
☎ (2) 40 63 16 02

06000 Nice
CONSULATE (HON)
2 rue du Congress ☎ (4) 93 82 32 04
(also deals with MONACO)

35800 St Malo/Dinard
CONSULATE (HON)
La Hulotte,
8 blvd des Maréchaux
☎ (2) 99 46 26 64

31300 Toulouse
CONSULATE (HON)
c/o Lucas Aerospace
Victoria Centre,
Bâtiment Didier Daurant,
20 Chemin de Laporte
☎ (5) 61 15 02 02

GERMANY
10117 Berlin
EMBASSY
British Embassy Berlin Office,
Unter den Linden 32/34
☎ (030) 201 840

53113 Bonn
EMBASSY
Friedrich-Ebert-Allée 77
☎ (0228) 9167-0

28199 Bremen 1
CONSULATE (HON)
Herrlichkeiten 6,
Postfach 10 38 60
☎ (0421) 59090

40476 Düsseldorf 30
CONSULATE-GENERAL
Yorck Strasse 19
☎ (0211) 9448-1
☎ (0211) 9448 238 (passports)
☎ (0211) 9448 271 (visas)

60323 Frankfurt-am-Main
CONSULATE-GENERAL
Triton Haus
Bockenheimer Landstrasse 42
☎ (069) 170002-0

20148 Hamburg
CONSULATE-GENERAL
Harvestehuder Weg 8a
☎ (040) 4480320

30175 Hannover 1
CONSULATE (HON)
Berliner Allee 5
☎ (0511) 9919 100

24159 Kiel
CONSULATE (HON)
c/o United Baltic Corporation
GmbH, Schleuse, Maklerstrasse
☎ (0431) 331971

80538 München
CONSULATE-GENERAL
Bürkleinstrasse 10
☎ (089) 211090

8500 Nürnberg
CONSULATE (HON)
c/o Schwan-Stabilo
Schwanhausser GmbH & Co.,
Maxfeld Strasse 3,
PO Box 4553
☎ (0911) 3609 522/521/520

70173 Stuttgart 1
CONSULATE-GENERAL
Breite Strasse 2
☎ (0711) 16269-0

GREECE
106 75 Athína (Athens)
EMBASSY
1 Ploutarchou Street
☎ (01) 7236211

841 00 Syros
VICE-CONSULATE (HON)
8 Akti P Ralli Hermoupolis
☎ (0281) 22232 or 28922

712 02 Iráklion, Crete
VICE-CONSULATE
16 Papa Alexandrou Street
☎ (081) 224012

491 00 Kérkira, Corfu
CONSULATE
2 Alexandras Avenue
☎ (0661) 30055

26221 Pátrai (Patras)
2 Votsi Street
☎ (061) 277329

851 00 Ródhos, Rhodes
CONSULATE (HON)
11 Amerikas Street, PO Box 47
☎ (0241) 27247 or 27306

541 10 Saloníki
CONSULATE (HON)
8 Venizelou Street,
Eleftheria Square, PO Box 10332
☎ (031) 278006 or 269984

382 21 Vólos
(temporarily closed)

HUNGARY
Budapest V
EMBASSY
Harmincad Utca 6
☎ (01) 226 2888/2046

ITALY
00187 Roma
EMBASSY
Via XX Settembre 80A
☎ (06) 4825441 or 4825551
(also deals with ALBANIA)

70121 Bari
CONSULATE (HON)
c/o David H Gavant & Sons
Shipping, Via Dalmazia 127
☎ (080) 5543668

72100 Brindisi
CONSULATE (HON)
The British School, Via de Terribile 9
☎ (0831) 568340

50123 Firenze (Florence)
CONSULATE
Lungarno Corsini 2
☎ (055) 212594 or 284133
(also deals with SAN MARINO)

16121 Genova
CONSULATE
Via XII Ottobre 2/132
☎ (010) 564833/5

20121 Milano
CONSULATE-GENERAL
Via San Paolo 7 ☎ (02) 723001

80122 Napoli
CONSULATE-GENERAL
Via Francesco Crispi 122
☎ (081) 663511 (3 lines)

10126 Torino
CONSULATE
Corso Massimo d'Azeglio 60
☎ (011) 6509 202/668 9829

34100 Trieste
CONSULATE (HON)
Vicolo Delle Ville 16
☎ (040) 302884

30123 Venezia
CONSULATE
Accademia, Dorsoduro 1051
☎ (041) 5227207 or 5227408

LUXEMBOURG
2459 Luxembourg City
EMBASSY
14 Boulevard Roosevelt,
PO Box 874 ☎ 229864/5/6 (3 lines)

MALTA
Valletta
HIGH COMMISSION
7 St Anne Street, PO Box 506,
Floriana ☎ 2331347

NETHERLANDS
Den Haag
EMBASSY
Lange Voorhout 10 ☎ (070) 3645800

Amsterdam
CONSULATE-GENERAL
Koningslaan 44, PO Box 75488
☎ (020) 6764343

NORWAY
0244 Oslo
EMBASSY
Thomas Heftyesgate 8
☎ (22) 552400

6001 Ålesund
CONSULATE (HON)
Farstadgarden, St Olavs Place,
PO Box 130 ☎ 70 12 4460

5001 Bergen
CONSULATE (HON)
Carl Konowsgate 34,
PO Box 872 ☎ 553 48505

9401 Harstad
CONSULATE (HON)
Standgate 7, PO Box 322
☎ 7706 4631

5501 Haugesund
CONSULATE (HON)
Haraldsgate 139, PO Box 128
☎ 5272 3033

4611 Kristiansand (S)
CONSULATE (HON)
Tollbodgaten 2, PO Box 300
☎ 38 02 24 39

6501 Kristiansund (N)
CONSULATE (HON)
Vageveien 7, PO Box 148
☎ 7167 5333

4001 Stavanger
CONSULATE (HON)
Prinsengate 12, PO Box 28
☎ 5152 9713

9001 Tromsø
CONSULATE (HON)
c/o L Macks Olbryggeri,
PO Box 1103
☎ 77 68 48 00

7003 Trondheim
CONSULATE (HON)
Sluppenveien 10,
PO Box 6004
☎ 73 96 82 11

POLAND
00556 Warszawa
EMBASSY
Aleje Roz 1
☎ (02) 6281001 - 5

PORTUGAL
1200 Lisboa
EMBASSY
Rua de San Domingos à
Lapa 37-1200
☎ (01) 3961191 or 3961147

9000 Funchal, Madeira
CONSULATE (HON)
Avenida de Zarco 2,
PO Box 417 ☎ 20161

9600 Ribeira Grande, Sao Miguel, Azores
CONSULATE (HON)
Quinta do Bom Jesus Rua Das Almas
23 Pico da Pedra Rabo de Peixe
☎ (096) 498115

8500 Portimão
CONSULATE (HON)
Largo Francisco A Maurico 7-10
☎ (082) 417800

4100 Porto
CONSULATE
Avenida da Boavista 3072
☎ (02) 61 684789

ROMANIA
70154 Bucharest
EMBASSY
24 Strada Jules Michelet
☎ (1) 120303 - 6 (4 lines)

SLOVENIA
61000 Ljubljana
EMBASSY
4th Floor, Trg Republike
☎ (61) 1257 191

SPAIN
28010 Madrid 4
EMBASSY
Calle de Fernando el Santo 16
☎ (91) 3190200 (12 lines)
CONSULATE-GENERAL
Centro Colon,
Marques de la Ensenada 16
(2nd floor) 28004 Madrid
☎ (91) 3085201

03001 Alicante
CONSULATE
Plaza Calvo Sotelo 1/2-1,
Apartado de Correos 564
☎ (96) 5216190 or 5216022

08036 Barcelona
CONSULATE-GENERAL
Edificio 'Torre de Barcelona',
Avenida Diagonal 477
(13th floor)
☎ (93) 4199044 (8 lines)
(also deals with ANDORRA)

48008 Bilbao
CONSULATE-GENERAL
Alameda de Urquijo 2-8
☎ (94) 4157600 or 4157711

07800 Ibiza, Ibiza
VICE-CONSULATE
Avenida Isidoro Macabich 45,
Apartado 307 (1st floor)
☎ (971) 301818 or 303816

35007 Las Palmas, Gran Canaria
CONSULATE
Edificio Cataluna, C/Luis Morote 6
(3rd floor) ☎ (928) 262508

29001 Málaga
CONSULATE
Edificio Duquesa,
Calle Duquesa de Parcent 8
☎ (952) 217571 or 212325

07002 Palma, Mallorca
CONSULATE
Plaza Mayor 3D
☎ (971) 712085 or 712445

Es Castell, Menorca
VICE-CONSULATE (HON)
Cami de Biniatap 30 Es Castell
☎ (971) 363373

38003 Santa Cruz, Tenerife
CONSULATE
Plaza Weyler 8 (1st floor)
☎ (922) 286863 or 286653

39004 Santander
CONSULATE (HON)
Paseo de Pereda 27
☎ (942) 220000

41001 Sevilla
CONSULATE
Plaza Nueva 8-B
☎ (95) 4228875/74

43004 Tarragona
CONSULATE (HON)
Calle Real 33 (1st floor)
☎ (977) 220812

36201 Vigo
CONSULATE (HON)
Plaza de Compostela 23
(6th floor) ☎ (986) 437133

SWEDEN
S-115 93 Stockholm
EMBASSY
Skarpögatan 6-8
☎ (08) 6719000

S-411 05 Göteborg
CONSULATE-GENERAL (HON)
Götgatan 15 ☎ (031) 151327

S-951 88 Luleå
CONSULATE (HON)
SCSAB Tunnplåt AB
☎ (0920) 92000

S-211 39 Malmö
CONSULATE (HON)
Gustav Adolfs Torg 8C
☎ (040) 115525

S-851 88 Sundsvall
CONSULATE (HON)
SCA Graphic Paper ☎ (060) 164000

SWITZERLAND
3005 Bern 15
EMBASSY
Thunstrasse 50 ☎ (031) 3525021/6

1211 Genève 20
CONSULATE-GENERAL
37-39 Rue de Vermont (6th floor) ☎
(022) 7343800

6900 Lugano
CONSULATE (HON)
Via Motta 19, via Nassa 32
☎ (091) 238606

Montreux
VICE-CONSULATE (HON)
La Chaumiére,
13 Chemin de l'Aubousset,
1806 St Legier, Vaud
☎ (021) 9433263

8008 Zürich
CONSULATE-GENERAL
and Directorate of British
Export Promotion, Dufourstrasse 56
☎ (01) 2611520-6
(also deals with LIECHTENSTEIN)

TURKEY
Ankara
EMBASSY
Sehit Ersan Caddesi 461/A,
Cankaya ☎ (312) 4866230/42

Antalya
CONSULATE (HON)
Ucgen Mahallesi,
Dolaplidere Caddesi,
Pirilti Sitesi,
Kat 1 Kilit Sauna Karsisi
☎ (242) 2477000/02

Bodrum
CONSULATE (HON)
Atatürk Caddesi
Adlive Solak 12/C PK535
☎ (614) 64932

Iskenderun
CONSULATE (HON)
c/o Catoni Maritime Agencies,
Maresal Cakmak Caddesi 28
☎ (326) 6130361-3

Istanbul
CONSULATE-GENERAL
Mesrutiyet Caddesi No. 34,
Tepabasi, Beyoglu, PK 33
☎ (212) 2937540 or 2937545

Izmir
VICE-CONSULATE
1442 Sokak No. 49,
Alsancak, PK 300
☎ (232) 4635151

48700 Marmaris
CONSULATE (HON)
c/o Yesil Marmaris Tourism
and Yacht Management Inc.,
Barbaros Caddesi No. 118
Marina, PO Box 8
☎ (252) 4126486

Mersin
VICE-CONSULATE (HON)
c/o Catoni Maritime Agencies SA,
Mersin Orta Okulu Sokak 3/B,
Cakmak Caddesi
☎ (324) 232 1248, 237 8687

YUGOSLAVIA
11000 Beograd (Belgrade)
EMBASSY/CONSULATE
Generala Zdanova 46
☎ (011) 645034/55/87

FERRY PORTS

GETTING THERE

FERRY ROUTES

BELGIUM
Ramsgate-Oostende 4 hr *Sally Ferries* (Ostend line) –
6 per day. Also jetfoil (Passengers only) 100 mins
Sally Ferries – 2-6 daily
Hull-Zeebrugge 14 hr *North Sea Ferries* – 1 per day
Dover-Zeebrugge *P & O Stena Line* – (contact ferry
company for details)

DENMARK
Harwich-Esbjerg 19½-20 hr *Scandinavian Seaways*
– up to 3 per week
Newcastle-upon-Tyne-Esbjerg 19½- 20 hr
Scandinavian Seaways – every 5 days

FRANCE
Dover-Calais 1½ hr *P & O Stena Line* (catamaran and
ferry) – up to 22 per day
1½ hr *Sea France* (contact ferry company for details)
Dover-Calais 35-50 min *Hoverspeed* Hovercraft/Seacat –
up to 14 per day
Folkestone-Boulogne 55mins *Hoverspeed* Seacat
– up to 6 per day
Newhaven-Dieppe (catamaran and ferry) 2-3½ hr
P & O Stena Line – up to 4 per day each
Plymouth-Roscoff 6 hr *Brittany Ferries* – up to 3 per day
(summer), up to 3 per week (winter)
Poole-Cherbourg 4¼ hr *Brittany Ferries* 2 per day
Poole-St Malo 8 hr *Brittany Ferries* (May-Sept) –
4 per week
Portsmouth-Caen 6 hr *Brittany Ferries* – up to 3 per day
Portsmouth-Cherbourg (day) 5 hr, (night) 7-8¼ hr
P & O European Ferries – up to 4 per day
Portsmouth-Le Havre (day) 5½ hr, (night) 7½-8 hr
P & O European Ferries – up to 3 per day
Portsmouth-St Malo 9 hr *Brittany Ferries*
– 1 per day (up to 2 per week in winter)
Ramsgate-Dunkerque 2½ hr *Sally Ferries* – 5 per day
(Service will cease Spring 1997)
Southampton-Cherbourg 5-9 hr *Stena Line* – up to 2 per day

GERMANY
Harwich-Hamburg 23 hr *Scandinavian Seaways*
– 3-4 per week
Newcastle-upon-Tyne-Hamburg 23½ hr *Scandinavian
Seaways* – every 4 days
Oslo-Kiel 19 hr *Color Line* – daily

SERVICES FROM IRELAND:
Cork-Brest 16 hrs *Irish Ferries* – 1 per week summer only
Cork-Cherbourg 17 hr *Irish Ferries*
– 1 per week summer only
Cork-Le Havre 21½ hr *Irish Ferries*
– 1 per week summer only
Cork-Roscoff 14 hr *Brittany Ferries* – 2 per week
Cork-St. Malo 18½ hr *Brittany Ferries*
– 1 per week summer only
Rosslare-Brest 15½ hrs *Irish Ferries*
– up to 2 per week summer only
Rosslare-Cherbourg 17 hr *Irish Ferries* – 1 per week
Rosslare-Le Havre 21 hrs *Irish Ferries*
– up to 3 per week

NORTHERN IRELAND
Cairnryan-Larne 2¼ hr *P & O European Ferries*
– up to 6 per day
Stranraer-Belfast 3hr *Stena Line* – up to 9 per day
Stranraer-Belfast 1½ hr *Hoverspeed* – up to 5 per day

REPUBLIC OF IRELAND
Fishguard-Rosslare (ferry) 3½ hr *Stena Line*
– up to 2 per day
Fishguard-Rosslare (catamaran) 1hr 39 mins
Stena Line – 4 per day
Holyhead-Dublin 3½ hr *Irish Ferries* – 2 per day
Holyhead-Dun Laoghaire 3½ hr *Stena Line*
– up to 4 per day
Holyhead-Dun Laoghaire (catamaran) 1 hr 50mins
Stena Line – 4 per day
Pembroke Dock-Rosslare 4½ hr *Irish Ferries*
– up to 2 per day
Swansea-Cork 10 hr *Swansea Cork Ferries*
– 6 per week

NETHERLANDS
Harwich-Hoek van Holland (day) 6½ hr, (night) 10 hr
Stena Line – 2 per day
Hull-Rotterdam (Europoort) 14 hr *North Sea Ferries*
– 1 per day
Newcastle-Amsterdam *Scandinavian Seaways*
15-17½ hr – up to 4 per week
*Sheerness-Vlissingen (day) 7½ hr (night) 9½ hr
Eurolink Ferries – 2 per day
*route under review in 1997

NORWAY

Hirtshals-Oslo 8¼ hr *Color Line* – daily (summer)
Kiel-Oslo 19 hr *Color Line* – daily
Hirtshals-Kristiansand 4¼ hr (day) 6½ hr (night) *Color Line* – 3-4 per day
Newcastle upon Tyne-Bergen 19¼-25½ hr *Color Line* – 3 per week (summer) 2 per week (winter)
Newcastle upon Tyne-Stavanger 17-27½ hr *Color Line* – 3 per week (summer) 2 per week (winter)
Newcastle upon Tyne-Haugesund 19¾-25¾ hr *Color Line* – up to 2 per week

SPAIN

Plymouth-Santander (from mid March) 23-24 hr *Brittany Ferries* – up to 2 per week
Portsmouth-Santander (winter only) 30-31 hr *Brittany Ferries* – 1 per week
Portsmouth-Bilbao 30-35 hr *P & O European Ferries* – 2 per week

SWEDEN

Harwich-Göteborg 23 hr *Scandinavian Seaways* – up to 3 per week
Newcastle-upon-Tyne-Göteborg 23-24 hr *Scandinavian Seaways* – 1 per week

FERRY COMPANIES

P & O European Ferries
Channel House, Channel View Road,
Dover CT17 9TJ ☎ (01304) 203388
Calais ☎ 03 21 46 04 40
Cairnryan ☎ (01581) 200276
Le Havre ☎ 02 35 19 78 50
Cherbourg ☎ 02 33 88 65 70
Felixstowe ☎ (01394) 604040
Portsmouth ☎ (01705) 827677
Larne ☎ (01574) 274321
Bilbao ☎ (94) 423 4477

Sally Ferries
Sally Line Ltd, Argyle Centre, York Street, Ramsgate, Kent CT11 9DS
☎ (01843) 595522
☎ (0181)-858 1127
Dunkerque ☎ 03 28 21 43 44
Oostende ☎ 59 55 99 54

Sea France
106 East Camber Bdg, East Docks,
Dover CT16 1JA ☎ (01304) 212696

Stena Line
Charter House, Ashford, Kent
☎ (01233) 647047

Calais ☎ 03 21 46 80 00
Cherbourg ☎ 02 33 20 43 38
Dieppe ☎ 02 35 06 39 00
Hoek van Holland ☎ 47 82 351

Hoverspeed Ltd
International Hoverport, Western Dock, Dover, Kent CT17 9TG
☎ (01304) 240241
Boulogne ☎ 03 21 30 27 26
Calais ☎ 03 21 46 14 14

Scandinavian Seaways
Scandinavia House, Parkeston Quay, Harwich, Essex CO12 4QG
☎ (01255) 240240
Esbjerg ☎ 75 12 48 00
Göteborg ☎ (031) 65 06 00
Hamburg ☎ (040) 3 89 03 71

Brittany Ferries
Millbay Docks, Plymouth PL1 3EW
☎ (01752) 221321
The Britany Centre, Wharf Road, Portsmouth PO2 8RU
☎ (01705) 827701
Caen ☎ 02 31 96 88 80

Cherbourg ☎ 02 33 43 43 68
Cork ☎ (021) 277801
Roscoff ☎ 02 98 29 28 28
Santander ☎ 22 00 00
St Malo ☎ 02 99 40 64 41

Color Line
International Ferry Terminal, Royal Quays, North Shields NE29 6EE
☎ (0191)-296 1313

Eurolink Ferries
The Ferry Terminal, Sheerness Dock, Sheerness ME12 1AX
☎ (01795) 581000

North Sea Ferries
King George Dock, Hedon Road, Hull HU9 5QA ☎ (01482) 77177

Irish Ferries
2-4 Merrion Row, Dublin 2, Irish Republic ☎ 010 3531 6610511

Swansea Cork Ferries
The Ferry Port, Swansea SA1 8RU
☎ (01792) 456116

TIME DIFFERENCES

In many European countries, local time is altered during the summer, as it is in the UK. Although most European countries are one hour ahead of the UK throughout the year, there is a period in October when European Summer Time has ended but British Summer Time has not.
Note: Bulgaria, Cyprus, Finland, Greece, Romania and Turkey are two hours ahead of Greenwich Mean Time. In Portugal, the time is the same as in Great Britain.

GETTING THERE

THE CHANNEL TUNNEL AND FERRY PORTS

THE CHANNEL TUNNEL

The Channel Tunnel is, in fact, three tunnels, 31 miles (50 km) long. The two outer tunnels carry railway tracks for the two main thoroughfares, one each way, with a connected service passage between.

The 'Le Shuttle' tourist service is a drive-on drive-off train operation carrying cars, caravans and motorcycles. Slip roads from the M20 near Folkestone and the A16 near Calais take cars direct to the terminals. Passengers pay at a toll-booth, go through frontier controls and load their cars on to the special carriages. The crossing takes 35 minutes including Customs, embarkation and disembarkation takes an hour. At peak times the operation has up to four departures every hour but is

down to one an hour in the quietest time of night. It is not possible to book space on a particular train, though you can pre-purchase a ticket. Eurotunnel hopes that no one will have to wait more than half an hour, even at the busiest time of year.

Vehicles load from the rear of 'Le Shuttle', and are directed to park in one of the carriages. During the journey, car passengers can stay in their cars or walk around the carriage. Motor cyclists travel in a special compartment, away from their vehicles. Each carriage is air-conditioned, sound-proofed and has access to a toilet. Screens show progress information.

'Le Shuttle' Call Centre ☎ 0990 35 35 35.

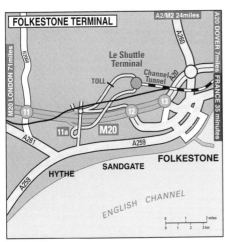

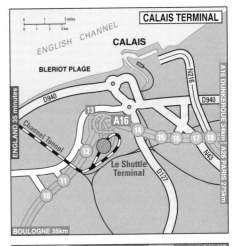

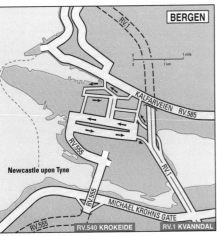

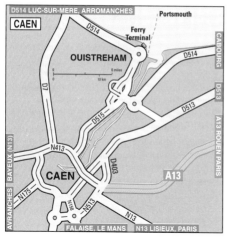

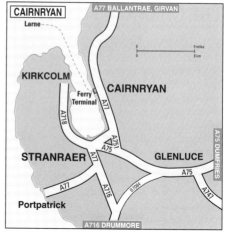

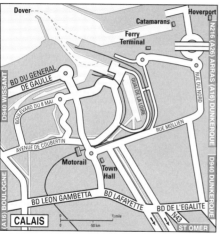

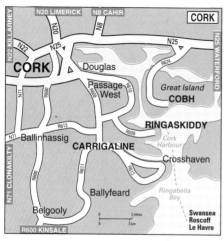

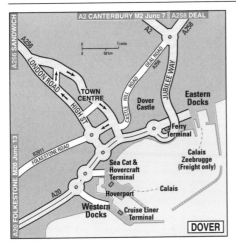

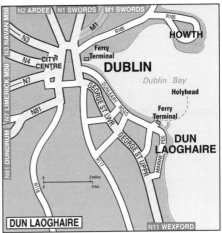

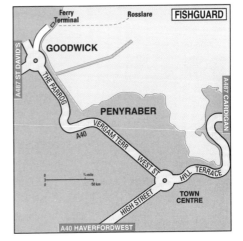

FOLKESTONE

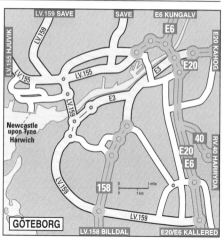

GÖTEBORG

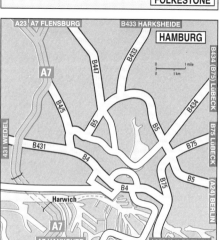

HAMBURG

HARWICH

HOEK VAN HOLLAND

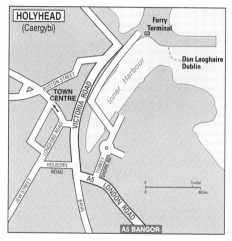

HOLYHEAD

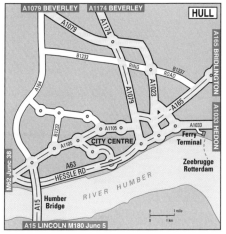

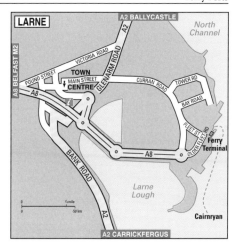

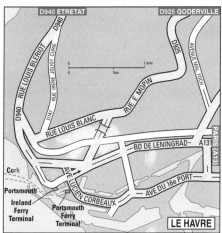

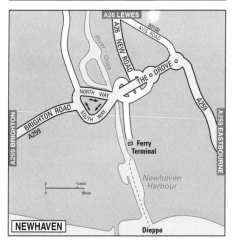

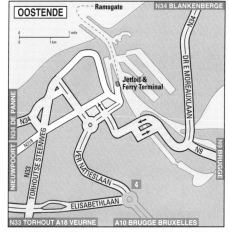

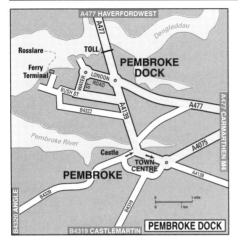

PEMBROKE DOCK

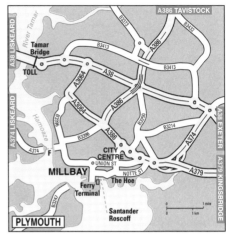

PLYMOUTH

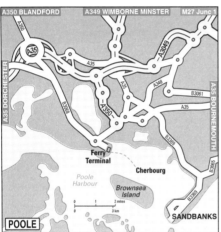

POOLE

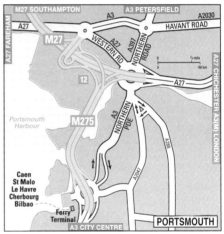

PORTSMOUTH

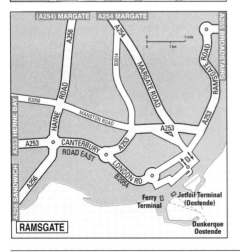

RAMSGATE

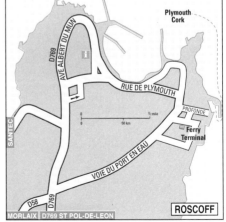

ROSCOFF

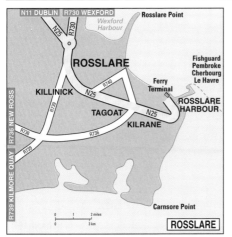

ROSSLARE

ROTTERDAM

ST MALO

SANTANDER

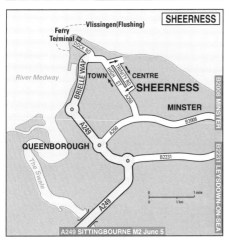

SHEERNESS

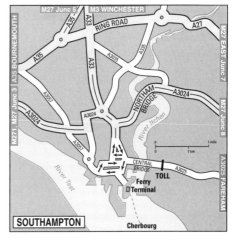

SOUTHAMPTON

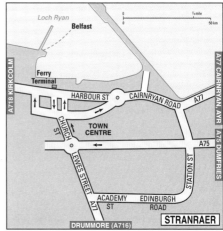

GETTING THERE

MOTORAIL

There are a number of advantages to travelling by Motorail including savings on petrol and on autoroute tolls, plus avoiding wear and tear on your vehicle and the stress of an arduous drive.

Motorail services are available from Calais and as well as Paris, Lille and Bruxelles. The following list shows some popular destinations and the approximate journey times.

AUSTRIA
Bruxelles-Salzburg, 12 hr.
Bruxelles-Villach, 15 hr.

FRANCE
Calais-Avignon, $11^{1}/_{2}$-$13^{1}/_{2}$hr.
Calais-Biarritz, $13^{1}/_{2}$ hr.
Calais-Bordeaux, $11^{1}/_{2}$ hr.
Calais-Brive, 9-10 hr.
Calais-Narbonne, $13^{1}/_{4}$-$14^{1}/_{2}$ hr.
Calais-Nice, $14^{1}/_{2}$-15 hr.
Calais-Toulouse, 12-$12^{1}/_{2}$ hr.
Lille-Avignon, $11^{1}/_{2}$ hr.
Lille-Biarritz, 10-$12^{1}/_{2}$ hr.
Lille-Bordeaux, $10^{1}/_{2}$ hr.
Lille-Narbonne, $11^{3}/_{4}$-$12^{1}/_{2}$ hr.
Lille-Nice, $14^{1}/_{2}$ hr.
Paris-Avignon, $7^{1}/_{2}$ hr.
Paris-Biarritz, 8 hr.
Paris-Bordeaux, $6^{1}/_{2}$-8 hr.

Paris-Briançon, $10^{1}/_{2}$-12 hr.
Paris-Brive, 7 hr.
Paris-Evian, $7^{1}/_{2}$ 10 hr.
Paris-Fréjus, $10^{1}/_{2}$-11 hr.
Paris-Marseille, 9-10 hr.
Paris-Narbonne, $10^{3}/_{4}$ hr.
Paris-Nice, 12 hr.
Paris-St Gervais, 9-11 hr.
Paris-Tarbes, 9 hr.
Paris-Toulon, $9^{3}/_{4}$ hr.
Paris-Toulouse, 9 hr.

ITALY
Bruxelles-Milano, 14-$14^{1}/_{2}$ hr.
Calais-Bologna, $17^{1}/_{2}$ hr.
Calais-Livorno, $16^{1}/_{2}$-$17^{1}/_{2}$ hr.
Calais-Milano, 12-$15^{1}/_{2}$ hr.
Calais-Rimini, $19^{1}/_{2}$ hr.
Calais-Roma, $20^{1}/_{4}$-$20^{3}/_{4}$ hr.
Paris-Bologna, 14-15 hr.
Paris-Milano, $10^{1}/_{2}$-11 hr.
Paris-Rimini, 15-$15^{1}/_{4}$ hr.

SPAIN
Paris-Madrid, $24^{1}/_{2}$-$28^{1}/_{2}$ hr.
Bilbao-Alicante $15^{1}/_{2}$ hr.
Bilbao-Malaga 14 hr.

DISTANCES FROM FERRY PORTS TO MAJOR EUROPEAN CITIES

* Distances from Boulogne are much the same as from Calais.

	SANTANDER	ROSCOFF	ST MALO	CHERBOURG	CAEN	LE HAVRE	DIEPPE
Amsterdam	-	-	-	-	-	361	299
Athina (Athens)	-	-	-	-	1448	1420f	1446f
Avignon	536	695	593	648	577	548	544
Barcelona	435	767	682	750	669	745	741
Berlin	-	-	-	-	-	-	-
Bern	-	-	-	-	-	470	460
Bilbao	65	615	529	597	580	612	630
Bordeaux	268	405	319	388	370	402	420
Brindisi	-	-	-	-	1304	1274	1266
Bruxelles	-	-	-	-	-	241	180
Den Haag	-	-	-	-	-	-	-
Dijon	-	-	-	-	342	314	310
Firenze (Florence)	-	-	-	-	859	831	827
Genève	-	-	-	-	485	455	451
Genova	-	-	-	-	721	692	690
Gibraltar	648	1258	1172	1240	1216	1255	1273
København	-	-	-	-	-	-	-
Köln (Cologne)	-	-	-	-	-	352	300
Lisboa	526	1153	1068	1135	1118	1151	1168
Luxembourg	-	-	-	-	-	355	291
Lyon	-	-	445	509	437	409	405
Madrid	237	847	761	829	811	844	862
Milano	-	-	757	756	682	652	651
München	-	-	-	-	-	-	584
Nantes	-	197	117	197	184	247	270
Napoli	-	-	1223	1222	1150	1122	1118
Nice	-	-	746	797	726	698	693
Oslo	-	-	-	-	-	-	-
Paris	-	-	252	224	153	124	107
Porto	398	1033	948	1016	998	1031	1048
Praha (Prague)	-	-	-	-	-	774	720
Roma	-	-	1104	1100	1028	1000	996
Stockholm	-	-	-	-	-	-	-
Strasbourg	-	-	-	-	-	-	372
Valencia	443	898	812	880	862	958	952
Venezia	-	-	-	-	846	817	815
Wien (Vienna)	-	-	-	-	-	-	859

f - includes a ferry crossing. These mileages are those by a good practicable route and are given as a guide only. It must not be expected that the mileage of a route provided by the RAC will necessarily coincide with the distance quoted here.

CALAIS*	DUNKERQUE	OOSTENDE	ROTTERDAM (EUROPOORT)	HAMBURG	ESBJERG	GOTEBORG	BERGEN	
229	211	176	66	289	451	616f	916f	Amsterdam
1482f	1947	1403f	1428f	-	-	-	-	Athína (Athens)
609	616	622	691	-	-	-		Avignon
864	870	-	-	-	-	-		Barcelona
581	572	523	450	180	347	411f	-	Berlin
480	536	474	501	569	739	921f	-	Bern
751	758	-	-	-	-	-	-	Bilbao
541	549	-	-	-	-	-	-	Bordeaux
1334	1341	1255	1278	1346	-	-	-	Brindisi
128	108	70	106	-	-	-	-	Bruxelles
211	188	153	33	-	-	-	-	Den Haag
357	364	369	-	-	-	-	-	Dijon
897	904	826	849-	-	-	-	-	Firenze (Florence)
515	522	527	600	-	-	-	-	Genève
751	758	725	748	-	-	-	-	Genova
1394	1401	-	-	-	-	-	-	Gibraltar
664f	647	611f	523f	199f	166f	157f	702f	København
258	238	204	174	263	-	-	-	Köln (Cologne)
1290	1296	-	-	-	-	-	-	Lisboa
261	241	208	233	-	-	-	-	Luxembourg
470	477	482	-	-	-	-	-	Lyon
983	990	-	-	-	-	-	-	Madrid
718	719	641	664	729	-	-	-	Milano
591	560	554	524	484	-	-	-	München
420	427	-	-	-	-	-	-	Nantes
1184	1207	1116	1139	1204	-	-	-	Napoli
759	766	771	-	-	-	-	-	Nice
1031f	1010	974f	-	-	-	199	312f	Oslo
180	190	193	-	-	-	-	-	Paris
1170	1177	-	-	-	-	-	-	Porto
722	706	659	608	412	582	-	-	Praha (Prague)
1062	1077	995	1018	1084	-	-	-	Roma
-	1034	-	-	574f	511f	360	665f	Stockholm
384	376	344	368	-	-	-	-	Strasbourg
1075	1081	-	-	-	-	-	-	Valencia
876	883	818	786	805	-	-	-	Venezia
858	841	795	735	713	-	-	-	Wien (Vienna)

EUROPE BY COUNTRY

In this section of the Guide, essential motoring
information and valuable general information is given
in detail for each individual country.

Driving in Europe can present many unfamiliar problems,
and advice on several of those likely to be encountered is
presented here by way of an introduction.

'BISON FUTE'

In France you will see signs for exits off the autoroutes
marked 'Bis' on an orange panel. This is short for *'Bison
Futé'*, and indicates alternative routes which avoid areas
prone to congestion at peak periods. A free map of 'Bis'
routes is published in June each year by the French
Government; contact RAC Travel Information
☎ 0345 333 222 or Maison de la France (see page 12).

DRINKING AND DRIVING

Many motorists believe that they are safe with a blood
alcohol level of 50 or 80mg: they are wrong. Even at a
level of 20mg, signs of impaired concentration may
register. Remember that factors like fatigue, illness or
stress have additional effects, and may cause severe
concentration loss even when only small amounts of
alcohol are consumed. Blood alcohol limits are given
for each country. Penalties for exceeding these limits
can be very severe. The limit in the UK is 80mg.

FUEL

Information on the availability and octane rating of
leaded and unleaded petrol, translations for unleaded
petrol, and regulations concerning the carriage of spare
fuel are detailed for each country.

The grades are shown as 'Regular' (the cheapest) and
'Super' (covering both 'Premium' and 'Super' grades in
Europe, which correspond to the two British grades).
The best guide to the grade is price. If you use 'Super' in
the UK, then use the most expensive abroad. Where
three grades are available, do not use the lowest unless
you are sure that your car will run on it. Where only one
grade is available, this is likely to be the equivalent of the
cheaper UK grade. The current prices of petrol and
diesel in European countries are available from
RAC Travel Information ☎ 0345 333 222.
If in doubt, contact the car manufacturer prior to
departure, or RAC Technical Advice ☎ 0345 345 500.
If paying by credit card, visitors are strongly advised to
check that the amount of fuel purchased tallies with the
figure on the voucher before signing.

LEVEL CROSSINGS

A level crossing is indicated by three roadside signals,
set at 80m intervals before the point where road and
railway cross. At the level crossing, approaching trains
are often indicated by a beacon flashing red
intermittently; this changes to white or amber when
there are no trains approaching. Some level crossings
do not have gates or barriers, and an approaching train
is indicated by a flashing red light or continuous bell.
Headlights must not be on when waiting at a level
crossing after dark.

MOUNTAIN ROADS

Strong winds can affect steering, and a firm grip on the
wheel is necessary. Even in summer, mist is not
uncommon at high altitudes. If you are unsure of your
position on a mountain, draw well into your own side
of the road, stop the car (keeping the lights on), and
wait until visibility improves.

Traffic descending should give way to that ascending.
Postal vans and coaches (usually marked with a bugle
sign) have priority, and any instructions given by their
drivers must be followed.

OVERHEATING

In hot weather generally, the level of water in the
radiator needs to be checked frequently. If the radiator
has lost water but the level is still above the bottom of
the header tank, water may be added immediately,
provided the engine is allowed to tick over and mix the
cold water with the hot water in the engine. If the
system has run dry, the engine must be allowed to
cool before water is added, otherwise the cylinder
block may be severely damaged.

If you suspect that the water in the radiator is
overheating, do not attempt to open the radiator cap
immediately. Allow the water to cool first.

High temperatures and prolonged ascents can cause
petrol to vaporise in the fuel lines, pump or
carburettor, and the engine will stop. If this happens,
allow the engine to cool; a damp cloth placed over the
engine will speed the cooling process.

OVERLOADING

Each passenger should have a fixed seat, and the
luggage weight should not exceed that recommended
by the manufacturer's handbook. Take care not to

overload the roof rack; Switzerland, for example, normally applies a 50kg limit to roof rack loads. In the case of an accident, the driver of an overloaded vehicle could be prosecuted and might find himself inadequately covered by insurance. The French authorities in particular, are concerned by the serious overloading of many British-registered cars touring France.

OVERTAKING

In Europe, one of the main problems for drivers of right-hand drive vehicles is overtaking, as vehicles in front block the view of the road ahead. It is necessary to keep well back from the vehicle in front in order to see whether it is safe to overtake. A mirror fitted on the left-hand side of the car will prove useful.

ROUNDABOUTS

These are often confusing for British drivers. In Germany, Sweden, Denmark and Norway, if there is a 'Give Way' sign, traffic on a roundabout has priority, as in the UK. In France, it is now normal for traffic on a roundabout to have priority: a triangular sign with a red border showing a roundabout symbol with the legend *vous n'avez pas la priorité* indicates this. However, in a few areas the old ruling of priority given to traffic entering a roundabout still applies. So, where the above sign is not present, you should approach with care.

In all other countries, traffic on a roundabout should give way to traffic wishing to enter.

SAFETY

There have been a growing number of reports concerning a modern form of 'highway robbery' on some trunk routes through **France** and **Spain**. Although such incidents are minimal in relation to the thousands of journeys made to those countries, it could be well worth bearing in mind that the seemingly friendly stranger – only too keen to hear about your planned route and destination – may be making some plans of his own.

Many countries in Europe have undergone change recently, both peaceful and violent. At the time of going to press, the Foreign and Commonwealth Office offered the following advice to intending travellers. **Bosnia and Herzegovina**: because of continuing hostilities, travel to Bosnia is inadvisable. **CIS**: civil unrest and Nationalist tensions simmer in many areas; parts of Azerbaijan, Moldova and Tajikistan (as well as Armenia and Georgia) are not safe for tourists.

Croatia: parts of northern Croatia are considered safe, but rapid deterioration of security is always a risk. **Slovenia**: the whole of Slovenia is considered safe for tourists. **Turkey**: terrorist activity renders travel hazardous in certain parts of the country. **Yugoslavia, Federal Republic of (Serbia and Montenegro)**: Contact the FCO for advice.

Travel information for all countries may be obtained from the Foreign & Commonwealth Office Travel Advice Unit, ☎ 0171-238 4503/4504.

AUSTRIAN VIGNETTE

As of 1 January 1997, a motorway tax disc must be displayed on all vehicles using motorways. Visitors may purchase a **weekly** (valid for a maximum of 10 days) or **monthly** (valid for 2 consecutive calendar months) disc at all major Austrian border crossings, petrol stations and post offices. Annual discs are also available. The cost, in Austrian Schillings, is as follows:

	2 month	weekly
motorcycle	80	not available
private car (with or without trailer), certain mini-buses	150	70
vehicle between 3.5–7.5 tons	1500	300

The disc is not valid on the following motorways, although a disc entitles motorists to a 15% discount on the toll: S16 Arlberg Tunnel, A13 Brenner Motorway, A9 Pyhrn Motorway, A10 Tauern Motorway.

The major Austrian toll road companies issue multiple journey cards which allow an appreciable reduction in the price charged for a single journey. An additional charge may be made per person for over two or three people in cars or minibuses but children travel at reduced prices, sometimes free. For further details see page 73.

SWISS VIGNETTE

In order to drive on Swiss motorways, motorists must buy a vignette. These can be bought at Customs posts, post offices, garages, etc in Switzerland, or in this country from the Switzerland Tourism in London. The vignette is valid for one year, must be displayed on the windscreen and is non-transferable. A separate vignette must be bought and displayed on a trailer or caravan. The Swiss advise travellers to buy them in advance to avoid delays and queues at border crossings; credit cards are not accepted for payment of a vignette. You will be fined 100 Swiss francs if you do not have one, plus the cost of the vignette.

ANDORRA

MOTORING INFORMATION
National motoring organisation
Automobil Club d'Andorra, *FIA*, Babet Camp 4,
Andorra la Vieja. ☎ 20-8-90.
Accidents and emergencies
Police ☎ 17, Fire Brigade, Ambulance ☎ 18.
Fuel
Leaded petrol: Super (98 octane) available.
Speed limits
Built-up areas: 25mph (40kmh); *outside built-up
areas*: 44mph (70kmh). The police are empowered to
collect on-the-spot fines.

GENERAL INFORMATION
Banks
Open Mon-Fri 0900-1300 & 1500-1700, Sat 0900-1300.

Currency
French francs and Spanish pesetas are used but
telephones and To make a BT Chargecard call to the UK
take one currency only.
Public holidays
Canillo, third Sat in July; St Julia de Loria, last Sun in July
and following Mon and Tue; Escaldos Engerdany, 25, 26
and 27 July; Andorra la Vieja, first Sat in Aug, and
following Sun and Mon; La Massana, 15, 16 and 17 Aug;
Meritxett Pilgrimage, 8 Sep; Ordino, 16, 17 Sep.
Shops
Open daily 0900-2000 (except 8 Sep).
To make a BT Chargecard call to the UK
Contact the local operator and ask for a Chargecard call
to the UK.

AUSTRIA A

MOTORING INFORMATION
National motoring organisation
**Osterreichischer Automobil, Motorrad-und
Touring Club (OAMTC), *FIA & AIT*,** Schubertring 1-3,
1010 **Wien (Vienna)** 1. ☎ 1-711 990. Office hours:
weekdays 0800-1700. Closed Sat/Sun and public
holidays, except the breakdown assistance service.
Accidents and emergencies
Police ☎ 133, Fire Brigade ☎ 122, Ambulance
☎ 144. These numbers are standardised throughout
Austria but the local prefix number must also be used.
Breakdowns
The OAMTC operate a Breakdown and Technical
Assistance service on major roads throughout Austria,
☎ 120 (24-hr Breakdown scrvice, Wien).
Caravans
Drivers of motorcaravans and towed caravans are
strongly recommended not to overload such vehicles.
The caravan weight should not exceed that of the
towing vehicle. Checks are undertaken at border
crossings to ensure this regulation is not infringed.
Carriage of children
Children under 12 and less than 1.5 metres in height are
not permitted to travel on the front seat, unless a special
seat or seat belt is used. Children under 12 but over
1.5 metres in height must use the adult seat belt.
Crash helmets
Compulsory for motorcyclists and passengers.
Drinking and driving
The blood alcohol legal limit is 80mg.
Drivers
The minimum age for drivers is 18.

Driving licence
UK licences bearing a photograph of the holder
accepted otherwise it must be accompanied by an
identity document with photograph, eg. passport.
EC licences (pink/pink & green) are accepted.
First aid kit
Compulsory.
Fuel
Most petrol stations are open 0800-2000, and many
operate 24 hours a day in large cities. *Leaded petrol*:
**Super has been withdrawn from sale. Super Plus
(98 octane), containing a special lead additive,
should be used by vehicles unable to take
unleaded petrol**. *Unleaded petrol:* Regular
(91 octane) and Super (98 octane) available; pump
legend *bleifrei normal* or *bleifrei super*. *Credit cards*:
rarely accepted as payment for fuel, apart from the
AVANTI chain who accept charge and credit cards.
Spare fuel: 10 litres of petrol in a can may be imported
duty free in addition to the fuel in the tank.
Hitchhiking
Prohibited on motorways and dual carriageways. In
Styria, Upper Austria and the Vorarlberg hitchhiking is
prohibited for people under 16.
Lighting
Dipped headlights are compulsory in built-up areas. No
parking lights are required if the vehicle can be seen
from a distance of about 55 yards (50 metres). If
visibility is bad, sidelights should be on. Mopeds and
motorcycles must use lights at all times.
Overtaking
Overtake vehicles on the left. Overtaking on the right is

permitted only when overtaking trams, in one-way streets, or when overtaking vehicles indicating left. Do not cross or straddle the continuous yellow line at the centre of the road.
Motorists should not overtake a parked school bus with flashing red and yellow lights.

Parking
Do not park in the following areas (except for a short wait of 10 minutes):
(a) At places indicated by 'No parking' signs.
(b) Where there are crosses on the roadway, in front of houses, entrances, or petrol stations.
(c) On narrow roads, on the left in one-way streets, or on priority roads outside built-up areas at dusk, in darkness, fog or any road condition which reduces visibility.
Do not park or wait where a sign says *Halten Verboten* (no waiting). In Baden, Bludenz, Bregenz, Feldkirch, Graz, Innsbruck, Klagenfurt, Krems, Linz, St Pölten, Salzburg, Schwaz, Wien, Villach and Wiener Neustadt, a fee is charged for motor vehicles parked in the Blue Zone. Motorists must buy parking tickets in advance from banks, tobacconists etc. The date and time of arrival must be indicated on the ticket and displayed on the windscreen. Unless otherwise indicated under the *Kurzparkzone* (short-term parking) road sign, parking is allowed for up to three hours. In other towns parking is free for up to 90 mins in Blue Zones. Parking tickets are not required but a parking disc must be used for all vehicles including motorcycles. This disc can be obtained free of charge from tobacconists. Do not leave a caravan trailer without its towing vehicle in a public parking place (eg motorway service area). In the Tyrol, Upper Austria and Salzburg, it is prohibited to park caravans outside specially authorised parking places or within 500 metres of a lake. Do not park caravans within 200 metres of the Grossglockner High Alpine Road and the motorway in Salzburg. Heavy fines and forcible removal of a caravan can result if these regulations are not observed.

Pedestrian crossings
In most large towns where there are traffic light controlled junctions without pedestrian lights, pedestrians may cross only when the lights are green for travelling in the same direction. Do not wait at the edge of the kerb.

Priority
Priority is given to main roads or those roads bearing the 'Main Road' symbol. On roads of equal importance, priority is given to traffic approaching from the right. Do give priority to trams coming from the left, also to police cars and all emergency vehicles with a flashing blue light and multi-toned sirens. When passing traffic on mountain roads, ascending vehicles have priority.

Road signs
Most conform to the international pattern. Other road

conditions may be indicated as follows:
Anhänger Verboten: trailers not allowed
Ausweiche: detour
Beschränkung für Halten oder Parken: stopping or parking restricted
Halten Verboten: no waiting
Hupverbot: use of horn prohibited
Lawinen Gefahr: avalanche danger
Querstrasse: crossroads
Steinschlag: falling rocks
Strasse Gesperrt: road closed

Seat belts
If fitted, compulsory use in front and rear seats.

Signalling
Give warning of approach by flashing headlamps. Horns may not be used where their use is prohibited by a road sign. This applies in many large towns, mostly at night, and in Wien at all times.

Speed limits
Built-up areas: 31mph (50kmh); *outside built-up areas*: 62mph (100kmh); motorways: 81mph (130kmh). Speed limits are lowered to 68mph (110kmh) between 2200 and 0500 hours on the following motorways: A8 (Innkreis), A9 (Pyhrn), A10 (Tauern), A12 (Inntal), A13 (Brenner), A14 (Rheintal).
Minimum speed limit on motorways and roads displaying a rectangular blue sign bearing a white car is 60kmh. Cars towing a caravan or trailer under 750kg are restricted to 62mph (100kmh) on all roads outside built-up areas, including motorways. If the trailer is over 750kg contact RAC Travel Information ☎ 0345 333 222 for guidance on speed limits.

Tolls
As of 1 January 1997, a tax disc must be displayed on all vehicles using Austrian motorways. For further information see page 73.

Traffic offences
Police are empowered to impose and collect on-the-spot fines up to AS 500. The police officer collecting the fine must issue an official receipt. The motorist may pay the fine during the following two weeks, and with the original paying-in slip, the fine is payable in most European currencies. Motorists refusing to pay, may request that the case be brought before a police court; however, the police may ask for a security to be deposited.

Warning triangle
Compulsory.

GENERAL INFORMATION
Banks
Open Mon-Fri 0800-1230 & 1330-1500 (Thu 1330-1730).
Currency
Austrian schilling.

To make a BT Chargecard call to the UK
Dial the BT Direct number 022 903 044 to contact a
BT operator in the UK, who will connect the call. Calls
can be made from Post Offices, Telephone Bureaux and
some payphones.
Public holidays
New Year's; Epiphany; Easter Monday; Labour Day;

Ascension; Whit Monday; Corpus Christi; Assumption,
15 Aug; National Day, 26 Oct; All Saints, 1 Nov;
Immaculate Conception, 8 Dec; Christmas, 25, 26 Dec.
Shops
Open Mon-Fri 0800-1830, with a one or two hour break
at midday. Sat 0800-1300. In central Wien shops do not
close for lunch.

BALTIC STATES

(EST)(LV)(LT)

MOTORING INFORMATION
National motoring organisations
Estonia: Eesti Autoklubi, AIT, 9 Rävala, 0001 Tallinn.
☎ (372) 6317 280.
**Latvia: Auto-Moto Society of Latvia (LR AMB), *FIA*
& *AIT*,** 16B Raunas, LV-1039 Riga.
☎ (371) 2 56 83 39, 56 62 22
**Lithuania: Association of Lithuanian
Automobilists LAS, *FIA* & *AIT*,** Lvovo 9, 2005 Vilnius.
☎ (370) 2 35 12 73, 35 21 86.
Accidents and emergencies
Police ☎ 02, Fire Brigade ☎ 01, Ambulance ☎ 03. When
an accident occurs, you must contact the police.
Breakdowns
The Finnish oil company, Neste Oy, provides a 24-hr
roadside breakdown assistance service, along the "Via
Baltica". The emergency numbers are :
(370) 2-53 43 86 or 53 42 91.
Drinking and driving
Do not drink and drive: blood alcohol legal limit is 0mg.
Driving Licence
UK driving licence accepted.
Ferries
Car ferry services operate on the following routes:

Estonia:	Operator
Helsinki (Finland) – Tallin.	*Tallink, Silja*
Stockholm (Sweden) – Tallin.	*Estline*
Latvia:	
Rostock (Germany) – Liepaja.	*Euroseabridge*
Lithuania:	
Kiel (Germany) – Klaipeda.	*Lita Shipping*
Mukran (Germany) – Klaipeda.	*Euroseabridge*

Fire extinguisher
Compulsory in **Lithuania** and **Estonia**.
First aid kit
Compulsory in **Lithuania** and **Estonia**.
Fuel
Availability of fuel has improved with the establishment
of a chain of 11 service stations by Neste Oy along the
M-12 ('Via Baltica') motorway.
These are located every 150km (90 miles) and are open
24 hours. Service stations may be found in Tallinn (2),
Parnu, Savikrasti (north of Riga), Riga (2), Kekava,

Panevezys, Marijampole and Vilnius (2).
Away from the Via Baltica, petrol stations are scarce, fuel
is of poor quality and the possibility of queues always
exists. Tankers selling petrol from lay-bys will be seen
along main highways.
Leaded: various grades are available, ranging from 75 to
98 octane. *Unleaded* : 95 and 98 octane grades available.
Quality fuel is available from Neste outlets.
Diesel: central European diesel fuel congeals in winter,
and motorists should purchase a special winter diesel
with a high congealing point, from Neste and Kesoil
stations. *Spare fuel*: up to 20 litres may be imported.
Payment : Neste service stations accept Visa, Eurocard
and Diner's Club. The Neste stations in Latvia accept
hard currencies: in Estonia, only Estonian Crowns are
acceptable; in Lithuania only Litas are acceptable.
Further information on the Via Baltica and fuel availability
is available from RAC Travel Information 0345 333 222.
Lighting
In **Latvia** and **Lithuania**, mopeds and motorcycles must
use dipped headlights at all times. In **Estonia**, all motor
vehicles must use dipped headlights day and night.
Parking
In towns motorists must take care not to park on tram
lines. Visitors should be aware that theft of cars and
contents is common. Guarded car parks should be used
whenever possible.
Estonia: There are a few parking meters in Tallin and
zones where tickets must be pre-paid and displayed on
the vehicle. Illegally parked cars will be clamped.
Lithuania: Parking is forbidden within 15m of a bus
stop and within 5m of a crossroads or intersection. There
are parking spaces in main towns. Clamps are not in use.
Road Networks
The major north-south route linking the Baltic States is
the 'Via Baltica' (M12), a hard-surfaced road 430 miles
(700 km) long from Warsaw to Tallin in Estonia. The
condition of roads in towns is poor with many potholes.
Outside towns the main roads are in good condition but
secondary roads are surfaced with gravel or sand.
Night driving
Visitors are not recommended to drive at night. Local
drivers tend to use sidelights only, and additional

hazards include slow-moving vehicles and obstructions caused by goods falling from vehicles.

Repairs
Spare parts for western makes of car are not available.

Seat Belts
The driver and front seat passenger must wear seat belts throughout the Baltic States.

Speed limits
Built-up areas: **Estonia** 30mph (50kmh), **Latvia** and **Lithuania** 37mph (60kmh), *outside built-up areas*: vehicles up to 3.5 tonnes – normal roads 56mph (90kmh), dual carriageways 68mph (112kmh). Visitors should be aware that fines will be imposed for minor speeding offences.

Temporary importation of vehicles
On arrival in the Baltic States, visitors must sign an undertaking to re-export the vehicle at the end of the stay. The declaration must be shown on leaving the country.

Traffic Offences
On-the-spot fines are levied in **Estonia and Lithuania**.

Traffic Restrictions
Motorists pay an entrance fee to enter the old city of Tallin, Estonia and the old town of Vilnius, Lithuania.

Vehicle insurance
Car insurance (does not include motorcycles) can be arranged in advance by Black Sea & Baltic General Insurance Co. Ltd, 65 Fenchurch Street, London EC3, ☎ 0171-709 9202/9292.

GENERAL INFORMATION

Accommodation
A range of accommodation is available in the main towns of Vilnius, Kaunas, Tallinn, Riga and Pärnu.
Accommodation may be booked through the Independent Travel Department, Intourist Travel Ltd, Intourist House, 219 Marsh Wall, London E14 9FJ, ☎ 0171-538 5965.

Banks
The following hours are a guide.
Estonia: Mon-Fri 0900-1500/1600
Latvia: Mon-Fri 1000-1430
Lithuania: Mon-Fri 0900-1230 and 1430-1700

Currency
There are no restrictions on the import or export of foreign currency at the time of going to press. Large amounts should be declared on entry to facilitate exportation. The importation and exportation of local currency is prohibited. Visitors are recommended to carry Deutschmarks or US Dollars in small denominations. Visitors are occasionally asked to settle bills in foreign currency. It is an offence to exchange money on the black market.
Estonia: Unit of currency is the Kroon (EEK) divided into 100 centimes. Money can be exchanged at banks, some hotels and the main post office in Tallin. *Credit*

cards: major cards accepted in Tallinn at major hotels, restaurants and shops.
Latvia: Unit of currency is the Lat, divided into 100 santims. Latvian Roubles are no longer legal tender. Money can be exchanged at banks and some hotels. *Credit cards*: major cards accepted in some hotels and restaurants.
Lithuania: Unit of currency is the Litas, divided into 100 cents. Exchange money at banks, some hotels and large shops and the main post office in Vilnius. 20 Lita notes are no longer acceptable as means of payment. The Tallon is no longer legal tender. *Credit cards*: in Vilnius, Visa cards accepted in some shops, restaurants, car hire companies and hotels. Elsewhere credit cards are only accepted in some large hotels and restaurants.

Customs
There are two border crossings from **Poland** into **Lithuania**: Ogrodniki, Poland (east of Suwalki) to Lazkijai, Lithuania and Szyplszki, Poland to Kalvarije, Lithuania on the Suwalki to Marijampole road. Vehicle queues are possible at both crossings caused by local traffic with goods to declare. It is acceptable for motoring visitors to drive past the queue to the border checkpoint for inspection of vehicle and personal documents by customs officials.

Language
Each country has its national language. Russian is generally understood, but may not be welcome.

Museums
In all countries, museums are usually closed on Monday and in some cases Tuesday as well.

Public holidays
Estonia: New Year's Day; Independence Day, 24 Feb; Good Friday; Victory Day, 23 June; Midsummer's Day, 24 June; May Day, 1 May; Victory Day, 23 June; Christmas, 25, 26 Dec.
Latvia: New Year's Day; Good Friday; St John's Day, 24 June; 11 Nov; National Day, 18 Nov; Christmas, 25, 26 Dec.
Lithuania: New Year's Day; Independence Day, 16 Feb; Restoration of Independence, 11 March; Good Friday; Mothers Day, 1st Sunday in May; Day of Mourning and Hope, 14 June; National Day, 6 July; All Saint's Day 1 Nov, Christmas, 25, 26 Dec.

Shops
Food shops usually open weekdays 0800-1400 and 1500 to 1700 (1900 or 2000 in Lithuania), Sat 0900-1500 (1800 in Lithuania). In Lithuania, department stores are open Mon-Fri 1000-2000 and Sat 1000-1800.

To make a BT Chargecard call to the UK
Contact the local operator and ask for a Chargecard call to the UK.

Visa
Not required by British nationals.

BELGIUM

MOTORING INFORMATION

National motoring organisations

Royal Automobile Club de Belgique (RACB), *FIA*,
53 rue d'Arlon, 1040 Bruxelles. ☎ (02) 2870911. Office
hours: weekdays 0830-1700.
Touring Club Royal de Belgique (TCB), *AIT*, 44 rue
de la Loi, 1040 Bruxelles. ☎ (02) 2332211. Office hours:
weekdays 0900-1800, Sat 0900-1200.

Accidents and emergencies

Police ☎ 101, Fire Brigade and Ambulance ☎ 100.
When an accident occurs, especially if injuries are
involved, police may insist that drivers undergo a blood
alcohol content test. Although in law a driver can refuse,
such refusal may result in his arrest. Belgian law also
requires all parties involved in an accident to remain at
the scene as long as required by police, and proof of
identity may be requested.

Carriage of children

Children under the age of 12 are not permitted on the front
seat unless an approved child restraint or child seat is used.

Crash helmets

Compulsory for motorcyclists and passengers.

Drinking and driving

The blood alcohol legal limit is 50mg.

Drivers

The minimum age for drivers is 18.

Driving licence

UK driving licence accepted.

Fuel

Most petrol stations are closed overnight from 2000 to
0800, and often all day on Sunday. Petrol stations on
motorways and main roads are open 24 hours a day,
including Sunday. *Leaded petrol*: Super (98/99 octane)
available. *Unleaded petrol*: Regular (92 octane) and
Super (95 octane) available; *pump legend normale sans
plomb, normale onglood, normale unverbleit* or
bodvrije benzine. Credit cards: major cards accepted at
most petrol stations on motorways and in large towns.
Spare fuel: 10 litres of petrol in a can may be imported
duty free in addition to the fuel in the tank.

Lighting

Use dipped headlights when travelling between dusk
and dawn, and when weather conditions are bad. Do
not use headlights as parking lights. Motorcyclists must
use dipped headlights during the day.

Overtaking

Do not overtake if vehicles are approaching in the
opposite direction; or at intersections, unless the road
used is marked as a main road or if the traffic is
controlled by a policeman or traffic lights; at level
crossings; where there is a sign prohibiting overtaking,
or if the motorist in front is about to overtake.

Parking

Limited parking zones ('Blue Zones') exist in major
cities and towns, where drivers must display a parking
disc on their vehicles on weekdays. Signs indicate the
entry and exit points of the zone. Discs are available
from the police, garages and certain shops. Outside a
blue zone, a parking disc must be used wherever the
parking sign has a panel showing the disc symbol.
Elsewhere, paid parking is controlled by parking meters,
automatic parking machines and 'cards'. In the case of
meters and machines located within Blue Zones, discs
must not be used unless the equipment is out of use.
Do not park within 50 feet (15 metres) of a bus, tram or
trolleybus stop or in the immediate vicinity of train and
tram lines crossing the road. Wheel clamps are used on
illegally parked vehicles in Antwerpen and Gent.

Priority

Priority must be given to traffic approaching from the
right, except when indicated by signs. Do give trams
priority over other vehicles.

Seat belts

If fitted, compulsory use in front and rear seats.

Signalling

Audible warnings may be used when necessary to indicate
your intention to overtake, but only outside built-up areas.

Speed limits

Built-up areas: 31mph (50kmh); *outside built-up
areas,* cars with or without trailers : 56mph (90kmh);
motorways: 74mph (120kmh).

Tolls

There are no motorway tolls in Belgium. A toll is
charged for the Liefenhoeks Tunnel in Antwerpen.

Traffic offences

Police are empowered to impose and collect on-the-
spot fines. For visitors, the fine for a serious offence is
5,600 BF. If the offender refuses to pay, a deposit will be
requested. Further non-payment can result in vehicle
seizure. Payment is accepted in a number of currencies
including £ Sterling.

Warning triangle

Compulsory.

GENERAL INFORMATION

Banks

Open Mon-Fri 0900-1200 and 1400-1600. Some banks
remain open at midday.

Currency

Belgian franc.

Public holidays

New Year's Day; Easter Monday; Labour Day; Ascension;

Whit Monday; Flemish National Day, 21 July; Assumption, 15 Aug; All Saints, 1 Nov; Armistice Day, 11 Nov; Christmas, 25 Dec.

Shops
Open 0900-1800 (Fri usually 0900-2100). Some shops close for two hours at midday, but stay open until 2000.
To make a BT Chargecard call to the UK
Dial the BT Direct number 0800 100 44 to contact a BT Operaor in the UK, who will connect the call.

BULGARIA   BG

MOTORING INFORMATION
National motoring organisation
Union of Bulgarian Motorists (SBA), *FIA & AIT*, 3 Place Positano, 1090 Sofia. ☎ 2 86 151. Office hours: Mon-Fri 0900-1800.

Accidents and emergencies
Police ☎ 166, Fire Brigade ☎ 160, Ambulance ☎ 150.
In the case of accident, if there is only minor damage to the vehicles, drivers may agree on the procedure to adopt without calling the police. However, if one of the drivers is not insured, the other driver is advised to call the police to draw up a report of the damage which he can produce to his insurance company. If the vehicles are seriously damaged, or if anyone is injured, the police must be called.

Carriage of children
Children under 12 years of age may not travel in the front seat.

Crash helmets
Compulsory for motorcyclists and passengers.

Drinking and driving
Do not drink and drive: blood alcohol legal limit is 0mg.

Drivers
The minimum age for drivers is 18.

Driving licence
UK driving licence accepted only with an official Bulgarian translation, otherwise an International Driving Permit is required.

Fire extinguisher
Compulsory.

First aid kit
Compulsory.

Fuel
Petrol stations are located in large towns and on main roads, at an average distance of 18-25 miles (30-40km). Some stations are open 24 hours but most open 0600-2130 daily. Motorists should buy fuel from blue pumps. *Leaded petrol*: Regular (86 octane) and Super (96 octane) available. *Unleaded petrol*: Super (93 octane) available; pump legend *bes olovo bleifrei*. *Spare fuel*: up to 20 litres of petrol may be imported. *Credit cards*: accepted at some petrol stations, eg Shell.

Lighting
In town, drivers must use dipped headlights if public lighting is insufficient or if conditions are poor. Sidelights may be used in well-lit streets. Foglights may be used only in case of fog, rain or snow, at the same time as sidelights.

Parking
In built-up areas although there are no parking meters or discs, blue zone parking operates using tickets. Stopping and parking are prohibited at places where they might obstruct traffic. These places are indicated by signs. In one-way streets, parking is on the right only. Outside built-up areas drivers should stop off the road on the hard shoulder and park at places indicated by the international 'P' sign.

Pedestrian crossings
Pedestrians have priority over all vehicles on zebra- type crossings, except trams. When crossing at an intersection, pedestrians already on the carriageway have priority over vehicles, again excepting trams.

Priority
At intersections without right of way, and T junctions, drivers must give way to vehicles coming from the right. Trams have priority over other vehicles approaching from right or left.

Roads
Main roads are numbered, and display international road signs, with distances in kilometres. Town names appear in both Bulgarian and French.
There are over 330 miles (530km) of motorways in Bulgaria. The 'Trakia' motorway (156km/96 miles) links the towns of Sofia and Plovdiv.

Seat belts
If fitted, compulsory use in front seats.

Signalling
Audible warning devices (horns) may be used *outside* large towns to prevent an accident. Places where the use of horns is prohibited are indicated by the international sign.

Speed limits
Built-up areas: motorcycle, car and trailer 30mph (50kmh), car, motorcaravan, 12 seat minibus 37mph (60kmh); *outside built-up areas*: motorcycle, car and trailer 44mph (70kmh), car, motorcaravan, 12 seat minibus 50mph (80kmh); *motorways*: motorcycle, car and trailer 62mph (100kmh), car, motorcaravan, 12 seat minibus 74mph (120kmh). All drivers are advised to reduce speed at night on poorly-lit roads. All drivers who have held a driving licence for less than two years must not exceed the following speeds – in built up areas

30mph (50kmh), outside built up areas 44mph (70kmh), motorways 62mph (100kmh).

Traffic offences

On-the-spot fines(with receipt) are imposed by police. Minimum fine 200 Leva.

Warning triangle

Compulsory.

GENERAL INFORMATION

Banks

In Sofia and main towns, usually open Mon-Fri 0800-1230 and 1300-1500, Sat 0800-1400.

Currency

Lev.

Public holidays

New Year's Day; National Day, 3 Mar; Easter Mon; Labour Day, 1 May; Education Day, 24 May; Christmas, 25 Dec.

Shops

In Sofia and main towns, usually open Mon-Fri 0800-1700, Sat 0800-1400. Some shops remain open all day.

To make a BT Chargecard call to the UK

Dial 123 to contact the foreign operator and ask for a BT Chargecard call to the UK. BT Chargecard calls can be made from payphones in the central Post Office.

Visa

A tourist entry visa (valid for three months) is required by British Nationals who arrange their own holiday and stay in Bulgaria for more than 30 hours. For visa application forms, send an sae to: Visa Section, Bulgarian Embassy, 188 Queens Gate, London SW7 5HL or ☎ 0171-584 9400/9433 (Visa section open Mon-Fri 0930-1230). Seven working days' notice is required. Motorists are recommended to obtain visas in advance of arrival at the border.

CIS ⟨ TJ ⟩⟨ TM ⟩⟨ RUS ⟩⟨ UA ⟩⟨ UZ ⟩⟨ KZ ⟩

The Commonwealth of Independent States (CIS) comprises Armenia, Azerbaijan, Belarus, Kazakhstan, Kirkghizia, Moldova, Russia, Tajikistan, Turkmenistan, Ukraine and Uzbekistan.

MOTORING INFORMATION

Accident and breakdown

In the event of accident or breakdown, motorists should obtain assistance from the nearest Intourist office or traffic police. An official accident report (*spravka*) should be obtained for presentation on leaving the country. Motoring visitors are strongly advised to carry a selection of spare parts for the vehicle as these may not be easily obtainable locally. Purchasers of European Motoring Assistance should consult their Assistance Document.

Drinking and driving

Do not drink and drive: blood alcohol legal limit is 0mg.

Driving licence

Each driver must have an International Driving Permit.

Fire extinguisher

Compulsory.

First aid kit

Compulsory.

Fuel

The standard grade of petrol is 76 octane, however, 95 octane petrol is available at a few outlets. Unleaded petrol is generally not available. Both petrol and diesel can sometimes be difficult to obtain. Petrol coupons have been discontinued and petrol must now be paid for either in hard currency or roubles. Visitors are advised to carry spare fuel with them as petrol stations

are, on average, over 62 miles (100kms) apart. Western brands of oil and anti-freeze are unlikely to be available so a supply should be carried from the UK.

Seat belts

If fitted, compulsory use in front and rear seats.

Speed limits

Built-up areas 37mph (60kmh); *outside built-up areas* 68mph (110kmh).

Motoring itinerary

Visitors must book accommodation and plan their route before departure (see *Visa* opposite). The visa should detail the visitor's full itinerary, and will not normally be issued directly to individual applicants unless booked through an accredited tour company.

Motorists require a special 'Autotourist' visa and an itinerary card. In addition, there is an official limit of 300 miles (500km) a day.

Itineraries may be arranged through the Independent Travel Department, Intourist Travel Ltd Intourist House, 219 Marsh Wall, London E14 9FJ, ☎ 0171-538 5965.

Other motoring regulations

Visitors are advised to travel during the day only. When night travel is unavoidable, dipped headlights only should be used. Do not stop in unauthorised places on roads where only transit travel is permitted. The horn should only be used in an emergency. Ensure the vehicle is in good operational order and not driven if a fault could endanger road users. It is an offence to have a dirty car.

Travel offences

Traffic police can impose on-the-spot fines for infringement of traffic regulations.

Vehicle insurance
British insurance is not valid in the CIS, and insurance cover may be taken out through the insurance agency (*Ingosstrakh*) – there are offices in various European countries. Cover may also be obtained on arrival at the frontier posts at Brest (Polish border) and Uzhgorod (Slovakia/Ukraine border).

Alternatively, insurance (does not include motorcycles) can be arranged in advance by Black Sea & Baltic General Insurance Co. Ltd, 65 Fenchurch Street, London EC3M 4EY, ☎ 0171-709 9202/9292.

Warning triangle
Compulsory.

GENERAL INFORMATION
Currency
Soviet roubles are still the official currency throughout the CIS. Visitors should take US dollars, ideally in small denominations, and should remember that the fluctuating exchange rate can alter prices considerably. Travellers' cheques are not widely accepted.

Language
Away from the main cities, a slight knowledge of the Russian language is beneficial. An ability to read Cyrillic is helpful in order to understand road signs.

To make a BT Chargecard call to the UK
Dial the BT Direct number 810 800 4977266 to contact a BT operator in the UK who will connect the call. The BT Direct number from Belarus to the UK is 8800 44. If ringing from Armenia, Azerbaijan, Kazakhstan, Kyrgyzstan, Moldova, Tajikstan, Turkmenistan, Ukraine and Uzbekistan, contact the local operator and ask for a BT Chargecard call to the UK.

Visa
Visas are required by holders of British passports, and are issued by the Consulate of the Russian Federation, 5 Kensington Palace Gardens, London W8, ☎ 0171-229 8027. (The visa section is open 1000-1230, except Wednesdays. Allow 14 working days.) For Ukraine, a visa is available from the Ukraine Embassy, 78 Kensington Park Road, London W11 2PL, ☎ 0171-727 6312. Visas for Uzbekistan and Tajikistan are issued at the border or by the relevant consulate in Moscow. Further visa information is available from Intourist in London.

In order to obtain a visa, visitors must plan their route and book accommodation before departure (see *Motoring itinerary* above).

CROATIA HR

MOTORING INFORMATION
National motoring organisation
Hvratski Auto-Klub, *FIA & AIT*, Draskoviceva 25, 41000 Zagreb. ☎ 41-454 433. Office hours: Mon-Fri 0730-1530 (Tue 1730).

Accidents and emergencies
In the event of an accident, the police must be called. A visitor must obtain a certificate from the police, detailing damage to the vehicle, in order to facilitate export of the vehicle from the country. Police ☎ 92, Fire Brigade ☎ 93, Ambulance ☎ 94.

Carriage of children
Children under 12 must not travel in the front seats.

Crash helmets
Compulsory for motorcyclists, motorcycle passengers and moped riders.

Drinking and driving
Do not drink and drive. The blood alcohol legal limit is 50mg. The police can carry out breath tests at random.

Drivers
Minimum age for drivers is 18 years.

Driving licence
UK driving licence accepted.

First aid kit
Compulsory (except motorcycles).

Fuel
Leaded: Super petrol (98 octane) available. *Unleaded*: 91 and 95 octane grades available. There are approximately 200 stations selling unleaded petrol. Most stations are open 0600-2000. Some of those on major stretches of road stay open 24 hours.

Lighting
Spare bulbs must be carried. Motorcyclists must use dipped headlights day and night. Motorists must use dipped headlights when visibility is reduced to 200 metres outside built up areas, and 100 metres inside built up areas, day or night.

Overtaking
Regulations as international practice. Overtake on the left, or on the right if the vehicle to be overtaken is turning left. It is prohibited to overtake a bus transporting children when passengers are getting on or off the bus.

Parking
Lines on the edge of the road indicate a parking prohibition. Traffic wardens control parked vehicles and impose fines for illegal parking.

Priority
Regulations as international practice. At intersections, drivers must give way to traffic from the right unless a

priority road is indicated. At roundabouts, vehicles must give way to traffic coming from the right, ie. vehicles entering the roundabout have the right of way. In built up areas, road users must give way to public transport vehicles and to specially marked school buses when these vehicles are leaving a stopping point.

Roads
There are three categories of roads – motorways (300 km), main road (4500 km), and minor roads (7900km). Hrvatski Auto-Klub (HAK) provides road trafffic information 24 hours a day ☎ 041 415 800.

Road signs
Road signs conform to the international pattern.

Seat belts
If fitted, compulsory use in front and rear seats.

Signalling
Do not use horns except in an emergency.

Speed limits
Built-up areas: motorcycle/car/car and caravan or trailer 37mph (60kmh); *outside built-up areas*: car, motorcycle 56-62mph (90-100kmh); *motorways*: 81mph (130 kmh); car and caravan or trailer 50mph (80kmh).

Traffic lights
The international three-colour system is in use.

Traffic offences
Police are empowered to impose on-the-spot fines for violations of traffic regulations.

Vehicle insurance
Dalmation and Istrian Travel Ltd provide insurance and compulsory Green Card cover for motorists to Croatia – Dalmation and Istrian Travel Ltd., 28 Denmark Street, London WC2H 8NJ. ☎ 0171 379 6249.

Warning triangle
Compulsory (except motorcycles). A vehicle with a trailer must carry two triangles.

GENERAL INFORMATION
Banks
Open Mon-Fri 0800-1900, Sat 0800-1200.

Currency
Croatian kuna. Foreign currency may be exchanged in bureax de change, banks and post offices. Bureaux de change operate in some hotels and at certain travel agencies. Exchange slips should be kept in order to convert unspent *kunas* on leaving the country.

Museums
Some museums are closed on Monday and on Sunday afternoon. Information from local tourist office.

Public holidays
New Year's Day; Epiphany 6 Jan; Labour Day 1 May; Constitution Day 30 May; 22 June; Assumption 15 Aug; Christmas 25 and 26 Dec.

Shops
Food shops open Mon-Sat 0600-1930; other shops open Mon-Fri 0800-2000, Sat 0800-1400.

To make a BT Chargecard call to the UK
Dial the BT Direct number 99 38 0044 to contact a BT operator in the UK who will connect the call.

CYPRUS

MOTORING INFORMATION
National motoring organisation
Cyprus Automobile Association, 12 Chr. Mylonas Street, Nicosia 141. ☎ 02-313233. Office hours: (June-Sep) Mon/Tue/Thu/Fri 0800-1300 and 1500-1900, Wed/Sat 0800-1300.

Carriage of children in front seats
Not permitted under the age of 5.

Crash helmets
Recommended.

Drinking and Driving
Suspicion of driving under the influence of alcohol may result in a blood test. Fines imposed.

Drivers
The minimum age for drivers is 18.

Driving
In Cyprus, drive on the left.

Driving licence
UK driving licence accepted.

Fuel
Leaded petrol: Regular (87 octane) and Super (98 octane) available. *Unleaded petrol*: available in major towns. *Spare fuel*: it is prohibited to carry fuel in cans.

Lighting
Lights must be used between half an hour after sunset and half an hour before sunrise. Spotlights are prohibited, but foglights may be used.

Priority
As a general rule, give way to vehicles coming from the right. However, traffic on main roads has priority at intersections where a 'Stop' or 'Give Way' sign is placed on the secondary road.

Seat belts
If fitted, compulsory use in front seats.

Signalling
Unnecessary use of the horn is prohibited, particularly from 2200-0600 and near hospitals.

Speed limits
Built-up areas: 31mph (50kmh); *outside built-up areas*: 50-62mph (80-100kmh).
Warning triangle
It is compulsory to carry two warning triangles.

GENERAL INFORMATION
Banks
Open Mon-Sat 0830-1200, and 1530-1730 for tourists.
Currency
Cypriot pound, which is divided into 100 cents.

Public holidays
New Year; Epiphany, 6 Jan; Greek National Day, 25 Mar; Easter (Greek Orthodox Calendar); National Holiday, 1 Apr; OXI Day, 28 Oct; Christmas, 24-26 Dec.
Shops
Open Mon-Fri 0800-1300 and 1600-1900 (winter 1430-1730), Sat 0800-1300. Shops close Wed afternoons.
To make a BT Chargecard call to the UK
Dial the BT Direct number 080 900 44 (Greek sector) to contact a BT operator in the UK who will connect the call. (not available from the Turkish sector)

CZECH REPUBLIC   (CZ)

MOTORING INFORMATION
National motoring organisations
Ustredni Automotoklub CR (UAMK), *FIA & AIT*, Na Rybnicku 16, 120 76 Praha (Prague) 2. ☎ 2-24 91 18 30. Office hours Mon-Fri 0745-1645.
Autoklub Ceské Republiky (ACR), *FIA*, Opletalova 29, 110 00 Praha 1. ☎ 2-24 21 02 66. Office hours Mon-Fri 0730-1600.
Accidents and emergencies
Police ☎ 158, Fire Brigade ☎ 150, Ambulance ☎ 155. If an accident causes bodily injury or material damage exceeding 1,000 Kcs, it must be reported to the police immediately. In the case of accident, where only slight damage occurs it is still advisable to report the accident to police who will issue a certificate to assist in export of vehicle.
Border crossing
All visitors must present their passports at an official border crossing post between the Czech Republic and Slovakia. However, there are currently no formalities for private cars.
Carriage of children
Children under 12, and persons under 4ft 9in (150cm), may not travel in front seats.
Crash helmets
Drivers of motorcycles over 50cc and their passengers must wear a crash helmet.
Drinking and driving
Do not drink and drive: blood alcohol legal limit is 0mg.
Drivers
The minimum age for drivers is 18.
Driving licence
International Driving Permit required.
First aid kit
Compulsory.
Fuel
Petrol stations on international roads and in main towns are open 24 hours a day. *Leaded petrol*: Regular (91 octane) and Super (96 octane) available. *Unleaded petrol*: Super (95/98 octane) available; pump legend

Natural. Maps showing outlets for unleaded petrol are issued at border crossings. *Diesel*: widely available. *Credit cards*: accepted at petrol stations in main towns and tourist areas.
Lighting
Foglights may be used in fog, snow or heavy rain. If the vehicle is not equipped with foglights, the driver must use dipped headlights in these conditions. Motorcyclists must use dipped headlights at all times. While waiting at level crossings, motorists must emit sidelights only.
Overtaking
Overtaking regulations conform with international usage. In built-up areas, when there are at least two lanes of traffic in each direction, drivers may use either lane. Trams are overtaken on the right. Only when there is no room on the right may the tram be overtaken on the left. In Praha it is prohibited to overtake trams on the left, the driver must follow the tram until he has enough room to pass on the right. Drivers must not overtake beside a tram refuge.
Parking
Vehicles may be parked only on the right of the road. If it is a one-way road, parking is also allowed on the left. Stopping and parking are prohibited in all places where visibility is poor or where the vehicle could cause an obstruction and, in particular, near an intersection, pedestrian crossing, bus or tram stop, level crossing and alongside a tram line unless there is still a 3.5m-wide lane free.
If visiting Praha, it is advisable to park outside the city centre and use public transport. It is forbidden to enter Wenceslas Square (*Vacavske namesti*) by car, unless you are staying at a hotel in the immediate vicinity. Vehicles illegally parked will be removed or clamped. Parking meters are being introduced in Praha and Brno. For further information, contact RAC Travel Information, ☎ 0345 333 222.
Priority
At uncontrolled crossroads or road intersections not marked by a priority road sign, priority must be given to

vehicles coming from the right. A driver approaching an intersection marked by priority road signs must give right of way to all vehicles approaching this intersection along the priority road.

Drivers may not enter crossroads unless their exit beyond the intersection is clear. A tram turning right and crossing the line of a vehicle on its right has priority.

Road signs

Most conform to the international pattern. Other road signs which may be seen are:

chodte vlevo: pedestrians must walk on the left

dalkovy provov: bypass

h nemocnice: hospital

jednosmerny provoz: one-way traffic

objì zdka: diversion

prujezd zakázáb: closed to all vehicles

Seat belts

If fitted, compulsory use in front and rear seats.

Signalling

Horns may be used only to warn other road users in case of danger or to signify that you are going to overtake. Warning may also be given by flashing the headlights. The use of horns is prohibited in central Praha 2100-0500 from 15 March to 15 October and 2000-0600 from 15 October to 15 March.

Speed limits

Built-up areas: 37mph (60kmh); *outside built-up areas*: 56mph (90kmh); *motorways*: 68mph (110kmh). Cars with caravan-trailer 50mph (80kmh). Motorcycles 56mph (90kmh) on all roads outside built-up areas.

Tolls

See page 74.

Traffic offences

On-the-spot fines of up to 2000 Kc in cash or 7000 Kc to be paid later may be imposed.

Warning triangle

Compulsory.

GENERAL INFORMATION

Banks

Open Mon-Fri 0830-1630. Closed Sat.

Currency

Czech crown ('Koruna 'ceska' Kc).

Museums

Open Tue-Sat 1000-1700. Closed Mon.

Castles

Castles are usually open from 1 May to 31 August. Open Tue-Sat, 1000-1600/1800. Closed Mon.

Personal safety

Visitors to Praha should be aware of the high incidence of petty theft. Pickpockets operate at the main tourist attractions, particularly the Charles Bridge, Prague Castle, Wencelas Square, Old Town Square and the Jewish Cemetry. Theft occurs frequently on trains, trams and at the main railway station. Passports and valuables should be left in a hotel safe. Carry small quantities of cash and a photocopy of your passport for identification purposes.

Public holidays

New Year's Day; Easter Monday; May Day; National Liberation Day, 8 May; St Cyril and St Method, 5 July; Johannes Hus Festival Day, 6 July; Independence Day, 28 October; Christmas 24,25,26 Dec.

Shops

Food shops open Mon-Fri 0800-1800, Sat 0800-1200. Department stores open Mon-Fri 0800/0900-1900 (Thu 2000), Sat 0800-1500.

To make a BT Chargecard call to the UK

Dial the BT Direct number 00 42 00 44 01 to contact a BT operator in the UK who will connect the call.

Visa

British Nationals no longer require a visa.

DENMARK $\qquad$ (DK)

MOTORING INFORMATION

National motoring organisation

Forenede Danske Motorejere (FDM), *AIT*, FDM-Huset, Firskovvej 32, Lyngby, København.
☎ (45) 45 93 08 00. Head Office hours: Mon-Fri 0900-1700, Sat 0900-1200.

Accidents and emergencies

Police, Fire Brigade and Ambulance ☎ 112.

Carriage of children

Children under three must be seated in a restraint system adapted to their size. Children over three may use a child restraint instead of a seat belt. Use of seat belts can be combined with use of a booster cushion.

Crash helmets

Compulsory for motorcyclists and passengers.

Drinking and driving

The blood alcohol legal limit is 80mg.

Drivers

The minimum age for drivers is 18.

Driving licence

UK driving licence accepted.

Fuel

Fuel availability is limited on motorways, and motorists are advised to fill their tank before joining a motorway. Petrol stations are often closed at night other than in large towns. There is an increasing number of self-service stations open 24 hours with pumps that require

100 DKK notes. *Leaded petrol*: Super (98 octane) available. *Unleaded petrol*: Regular (92 octane), Super (95 and 98 octane) available; pump legend *blyfri benzin*. *Credit cards*: major cards accepted at larger petrol stations. *Spare fuel*: a full can may be imported if entering from an EU country.

Internal ferries
Car ferries link the Jutland peninsula with the island of Sealand and the Danish capital, København. A frequent service operates across the Store Belt between Knudshoved on Funen and Halsskov on Sealand. The crossing takes one hour. For advance reservations, contact Scandinavian Seaways ☎ 01255 240240. A frequent car ferry service operates from Puttgarden, Germany to Rodby, Denmark providing road and bridge connections to København. A leaflet on international and internal ferry services is available from the Danish Tourist Board.

Lighting
Dipped headlamps must be used at all times.

Parking
In central København, in addition to restrictions indicated by signs, parking discs are required where there are no parking meters. Disc parking is usually restricted to one hour. At meters, parking is allowed for up to three hours. They are in use weekdays 0900-1800 and on Saturdays 0900-1300. 1 Kr and 25 Ore coins are used. In other large towns, kerbside parking is usually restricted to one hour. Discs are available from tourist offices, banks, post offices, petrol stations, and FDM offices. Do not park where there is a sign *Parkering forbudt*, or stop where signed *Stopforbudt*. Unlawful parking will result in the police towing the vehicle away. The vehicle will be released only upon payment of a fine.

Priority
Give way to traffic from the right except at roundabouts, where traffic already on the roundabout has priority. Do give way to traffic on a major road at a line of triangles painted across the carriageway or at a triangular 'Give Way' sign, and also to buses. Do not turn right at a red light, even if the road is clear, unless a green arrow indicates that you may. At junctions give way to cyclists and motorcyclists moving ahead when you are turning. When turning right, watch out for cyclists approaching from behind.

Road signs
Most conform to the international pattern. Other road signs are:
Ensrettet korsel: one-way street
Fare: danger
Farligt sving: dangerous bend
Fodgaengerovergang: pedestrian crossing
Gennemkorsel forbudt: no through road
Hold til hojre: keep to the right
Hold till venstre: keep to the left
Indkorsel forbudt: no entry

Korsvej: crossroads
Omkorsel: diversion
Parkering forbudt: no parking
Vejarbejde: road up
Vejen er spaerret: road closed

Level crossings
Drivers must reduce speed when approaching level crossings. Side lights only should be used at night when waiting at level crossings.

Mirrors
Right-hand drive vehicles must be equipped with exterior side mirrors on either side of the vehicle.

Seat belts
If fitted, compulsory use on all seats.

Signalling
Do not use your horn except in case of danger. Flash your lights instead.

Speed limits
Built-up areas: 31mph (50kmh); *outside built-up areas*: 50mph (80kmh); *motorways*: 68mph (110kmh); cars towing a caravan or trailer 44mph (70kmh).

Traffic offences
Danish police are authorised to impose and collect on-the-spot fines. If the visitor does not accept the fine, the case will be taken to court. The vehicle can be impounded until the matter is resolved and fines paid.

Motorways
No tolls are levied on the 400 mile (650km) motorway network in Denmark. Service areas, open from 0700-2200, are located at 30 mile (50km) intervals providing toilet, cafeteria facilities and travel information. Petrol stations are sited at similar intervals, on or just off the motorway, some have a cafeteria and shop. They are generally open 0700-2200 with automatic pumps for overnight use. Lay-bys are also located along motorways but do not have toilet facilities.

Warning triangle
Compulsory.

GENERAL INFORMATION
Banks
Open Mon-Wed, Fri 0930-1600. Thu 0930-1800, Closed Sat.
Currency
Kroner.
Medical treatment
Medical pharmacies are called *Apotek* and in Danish towns a number of these operate a 24-hour service.
Public holidays
New Year's Day; Maundy Thursday; Good Friday; Easter Monday; Constitution Day, 5 June; Ascension; Whit Monday; Christmas 24, 25, 26 and 31 Dec.
Shops
København: open Mon-Thu 0900-1730, Fri 0900-1900/2000, Sat 0900-1300/1400.

Provinces: open Mon-Thu 0900-1730, Fri 0900-1730/1900, Sat 0900-1200/1300. Larger stores: open Mon-Fri 0900-1800/1900, Sat 0900-1200/1400.

FINLAND   FIN

MOTORING INFORMATION
National motoring organisation
Autoliitto Automobile and Touring-Club of Finland (AL), *FIA & AIT*, Hämeentie 105, 00550 Helsinki 0050. ☎ 0-774 761. Office hours: Mon 0830-1730, Tue-Fri 0830-1600.

Accidents and emergencies
Police ☎ 10022, Fire Brigade and Ambulance ☎ 112. If you have an accident, report it to the Finnish Motor Insurance Bureau: Liikennevakuutusyhdistys, Bulevardi 28, 00120 Helsinki 12, ☎ (9) 019251.

Carriage of children
Children must be restrained either with a seat belt or in a child seat.

Crash helmets
Compulsory for motorcyclists and passengers.

Drinking and driving
The blood alcohol legal limit is 50mg.

Drivers
The minimum age for drivers is 18.

Driving licence
UK driving licence accepted.

Fuel
Petrol stations are usually open 0700-2100 weekdays, shorter hours at weekends. Some petrol stations are open 24 hours. There are automatic pumps which operate upon insertion of bank notes. *Leaded petrol* has been withdrawn from sale at certain outlets and replaced with an unleaded petrol grade containing special additive. *Unleaded petrol*: Regular (95 octane) and Super (98 octane) available; pump legend *ljyton polttaine*. *Credit cards*: accepted at most petrol stations. *Spare fuel*: there is no limit on the amount of fuel imported by visitors from other EU countries provided it is for personal use.

Lighting
Outside built-up areas all motor vehicles must use their headlights at all times.

Overtaking
Overtake on the left, unless the vehicle to be overtaken is signalling to turn left. In parallel lines of traffic, vehicles may be overtaken on the right. Vehicles being overtaken should not cross the white line which indicates the lane for cyclists and pedestrians.

Parking
Stopping and parking prohibitions follow international practice. Parking meters are usually grey and operate for between 15 minutes and four hours. Parking lights must be used if the parking place is not sufficiently lit. Although wheel clamps are not in use, police may remove illegally parked vehicles, and levy a fine.

Priority
At intersections, vehicles coming from the right have priority except on main roads. The approach to these main roads is indicated by a sign with a red triangle on a yellow background. When this sign is supplemented by a red octagon with 'STOP' in the centre of the sign, vehicles must stop before entering the intersection. Trams and emergency vehicles, even when coming from the left, always have priority over other vehicles.

Road signs
Most signs conform to international pattern. Some examples of written signs are:
Lossi-farja: ferry
Tulli: customs
Aja hitaasti: drive slowly
Tie rakenteilla: road under construction
Päällystetyötä: road resurfacing
Kunnossapitotyö: road repairs
Aluerajoitus: local speed limit.

Seat belts
If fitted, compulsory use in front seats.

Signalling
It is prohibited to sound a horn in towns and villages except in cases of immediate danger. *Outside built-up areas* horns and headlights should be used when and wherever visibility is not perfect.

Speed limits
Built-up areas: 31mph (50kmh); *outside built-up areas*: 50-62mph (80-100kmh); *motorways*: 74mph (120kmh). Cars towing a caravan or trailer are limited to 50mph (80kmh).

Traffic offences
Police are empowered to impose on-the-spot fines but not authorised to collect them. Fines should be paid at banks and post offices. Minimum fine – 150 FIM.

Warning triangle
Advisable.

GENERAL INFORMATION
Banks
Open Mon-Fri 0915-1615. Exchange offices are open longer hours, especially at Helsinki airport and ports.

Currency
Markka (FIM or Finnish mark).
Public holidays
New Year's Day; Epiphany; Good Friday; Easter Monday; May Day; first Sat after Ascension; Whit Saturday; All Saints, first Sat in Nov; Independence Day, 6 Dec; Christmas Day; St Stephen's Day. Other days are Vappu night, 30 Apr (a student and spring festival). Midsummer, 24 June is celebrated throughout Finland on the

Saturday nearest to 24 June with bonfires and dancing.
Shops
Open Mon-Fri 0900-1700, Sat 0900-1400/1600 according to season, and there are local variations. Shops at Helsinki railway and Metro stations are open Mon-Sat 1000-2200, Sun 1200-2200.
To make a BT Chargecard call to the UK
Dial the BT Direct number 9800 1 0440 to contact a BT operator in the UK who will connect the call.

FRANCE   F

MOTORING INFORMATION
National motoring organisations
Automobile Club de France, *FIA*, 6-8 Place de la Concorde, 75008 Paris. ☎ 1-43 12 43 12. Office hours: Mon-Fri 0900-1800.
Automobile Club National (ACN), *FIA & AIT*, 5 rue Auber, 75009 Paris. ☎ 44 51 53 99. Office hours: Mon-Thurs 0900-1300 and 1400-1800 (Fri 1700).
Accidents and emergencies
Police ☎ 17, Fire Brigade ☎ 18. Ambulance ☎ 17.
Breakdowns
Orange emergency telephones are situated every 2km along autoroutes and main roads.
Carriage of children
Children under 10 years of age must be seated on the rear seat of the car and use seat belts or child seat safety restraints adapted to their size. The only exception to this are babies or a very young child using approved rear-facing child seats.
Crash helmets
Compulsory for motorcyclists and passengers.
Documents
The French police can ask to see the vehicle registration document and driving licence. Motorists unable to produce documents immediately are liable to a 75F fine. If they are not presented at a police station within 5 days, a further 900F fine is liable.
Drinking and driving
The blood alcohol legal limit is 50mg.
Drivers
The minimum age for drivers is 18 (see **Speed limits**).
Driving licence
UK driving licence accepted.
Fuel
Leaded petrol: Super (98 octane) available. *Unleaded petrol:* Super (95/98 octane) available; pump legend *essence sans plomb. Diesel:* sold at pumps marked 'gas-oil' or 'gaz-oil'. *Credit cards:* major credit cards accepted. *Spare fuel:* up to 10 litres of spare fuel may be imported in cans.

Internal ferries
Car ferry services operate across the Gironde estuary between Royan and Le Verdon, and in the south between Blaye and Lamasque. Crossing time is 30 minutes and 25 minutes respectively. Services operate during daylight hours throughout the year.
Lighting
Headlight beams must be adjusted for right-hand drive vehicles. Beam converter sets, which can be fitted quickly and easily, are obtainable from the RAC. There is now no legal requirement for vehicles to emit a yellow beam. It is compulsory to use headlights at night in all areas, but these must be dipped in built-up areas. Motorcycle headlights are compulsory, day and night.
Do use headlights in poor visibility. Parking lights are obligatory, unless public lighting is sufficient for the vehicle to be seen distinctly from an adequate distance. A single offside parking light is permissible, provided the light is illuminated on the side nearest the traffic. If a driver 'flashes' you he expects you to pull to one side and let him pass.
Visiting motorists are recommended to carry a set of spare bulbs for the front lights, rear lights, stop lights and direction indicator lights.
Overloading
The French authorities are concerned by the serious overloading of many British-registered cars touring in France. Apart from the possible danger to all passengers, if involved in an accident the driver could well be prosecuted or held responsible for the accident by carrying more passengers and/or excessive weight than the vehicle manufacturer recommends.
Overtaking
Do not overtake where the road is marked with one or two continuous unbroken lines or when a vehicle is already being overtaken, or when a tram is stationary with passengers alighting or boarding. Processions, funerals or troops must not be overtaken at over 18mph. You may overtake, giving the correct signal, where the road is marked by broken lines, although the

line may only be crossed for the time taken to pass. A tram in motion may be overtaken on the right only, but on the left in a one-way street if there is sufficient space.

Parking

The usual restrictions on parking operate as in the UK with the following additions:
(a)   Do not park where the kerbs are marked with yellow paint or where you will cause an obstruction.
(b)   On roads outside town limits you must pull off the highway. Unilateral parking on alternate days is indicated by signs *Coté du Stationnement, jours pairs* – even (or *impairs* – odd).

In narrow streets in Paris, where parking both sides would obstruct the passage of double line traffic, this regulation applies automatically. Parking is prohibited in Paris along two main access routes designated *axes rouges* (red routes). The east-west route includes the left banks of the Seine and the Quai de la Mégisserie; the north-south route includes the Avenue du Général Leclerc, part of the Boulevard St Michel, the rue de Rivoli, boulevards Sébastopol, Strasbourg, Barbès, Ornano, rue Lafayette and Avenue Jean Jaurès.

Do not leave a parked vehicle in the same place in Paris for more than 24 consecutive hours. This restriction also applies in Hauts-de-Seine, Seine-St Denis and Val de Marne.

In Paris and the larger cities, there are Blue Zones, where parking discs must be used. They may be obtained from police stations, tourist offices and some shops. When a kerbside space has been found, the disc must be displayed on the windscreen and the clock set showing both the time of arrival and when the parking space will be free. Parking is limited to 1½ hours 0900-1900 (except between 1130 and 1430). Discs are not required on Sundays and public holidays. In other places, parking is shown by the international parking signs on which particular regulations are shown in black letters on a white background.

In some towns and cities, parking discs have been replaced with meters and pay and display schemes (*horodateurs*).

In Paris and some other large towns, illegally parked vehicles will be clamped or towed away. The vehicle will be released only upon payment of a fine.

Priority

The *priorité à droite* for all roads no longer holds. Traffic on major roads now has priority. Where two major roads cross, the sign *Danger Priorité à Droite* is used, indicating that traffic coming from the right has priority. *Passage protégé* (priority road) signs indicate those major roads where traffic has priority. In the absence of signs, give way to traffic coming from the right. Since 1984 traffic already on a roundabout has priority, and a triangular sign with a red border

showing a roundabout symbol with the legend *vous n'avez pas la priorité* indicates this. However, in a few areas the old ruling of priority given to traffic entering the roundabout still applies. So, where the signs are not present, you should approach with care.

Road signs

Conform to the international pattern but other road signs are:

Allumez vos lanternes: switch on your lights
Attention au feu: fire hazard
Attention travaux: beware roadworks
Barrière de dégel: applies to lorries when ice is thawing and roads are closed to lorries to prevent deterioration of road surface
Chaussée déformée: uneven road surface
Fin d'interdiction de stationner: end of prohibited parking
Gravillons: loose chippings
Haute tension: electrified line
Interdit aux piétons: forbidden to pedestrians
Nids de poules: potholes
Rappel: remember (displayed on speed limit signs)
Route barrée: road closed

Seat belts

If fitted, compulsory use in front and rear seats.

Signalling

Do not use horns except in an emergency.

Speed limits

Motorcycles over 80cc, private cars, vehicles towing a caravan or trailer with total weight under 3.5 tonnes: in built-up areas the speed limit is 31mph (50kmh), but this can be raised to 44mph (70kmh) on important through roads as indicated by signs; outside built-up areas on normal roads 56mph (90kmh); priority roads and toll free urban motorways 68mph (110kmh); toll motorways 81mph (130kmh).

Cars towing a caravan or trailer with total weight exceeding 3.5 tonnes: outside built-up areas the speed limit is 50mph (80kmh) on normal roads; priority roads 50mph (80kmh), but increased to 62mph (100kmh) on dual carriageways and to 68mph (110kmh) on motorways. Special speed limits apply if the trailer weight is more than the towing vehicle – the RAC can supply further information. On the Paris *Périphérique* ring road the speed limit is 50mph (80kmh). A minimum speed limit of 50mph (80kmh) applies for vehicles in the left lane of motorways.

In rain and bad weather, speed limits are lowered to: motorways 68mph (110kmh); dual carriageways 62mph (100kmh); other roads *outside built-up areas* 50mph (80kmh).

Visitors who have held a licence for less than two years are limited to 50mph (80kmh) on normal roads; 62mph (100kmh) on urban motorways and 68mph

(110kmh) on toll motorways. The speed limit does not have to be displayed on the vehicle.

Tolls
Payable on the autoroute network (see page 74). Tolls are also payable on the following bridges: from the mainland (west coast) onto Ile de Ré and Ile de Noirmoutier; Pont de Martrou, Rochefort (Charente Maritime); Pont de St Nazaire (Loire Atlantique); Pont de Brotonne (Seine Maritime).

Traffic lights
As in Britain except there is no amber light after the red light. Flashing amber means proceed with caution. Flashing red means no entry. Flashing yellow arrows mean the drivers may proceed in direction indicated, but must give way to pedestrians and the traffic flow they are joining.

Traffic offences
Some French police are authorised to impose and collect fines of up to 2,500F on the spot from drivers who violate traffic regulations. An official receipt should be requested.
If a minor offence is committed, a reduced fine is payable within 30 days. A court hearing must be arranged if the fine is to be contested. A guarantee must be deposited if a serious offence is committed by a

non-resident which is likely to result in a heavy fine and suspension of driving licence or prison sentence.

Warning triangle
Recommended.

GENERAL INFORMATION
Banks
Open weekdays 0900-1200 & 1400-1600. Some provincial banks open Tue-Sat 0900-1200 & 1400-1600.

Currency
French franc.

Museums
Most museums are closed Monday.

Public holidays
New Year's Day; Easter Monday; Labour Day; VE Day, 8 May; Ascension; Whit Monday; Bastille Day, 14 July; Assumption, 15 Aug; All Saints, 1 Nov; Armistice Day, 11 Nov; Christmas, 25 Dec.

Shops
Often closed Mon, all or half day, and for lunch two hours daily. Food shops are open Sunday morning.

To make a BT Chargecard call to the UK
Dial 19 02 44 for the automatic BT Chargecard dialling service.

GERMANY   D

MOTORING INFORMATION
National motoring organisations
Allgemeiner Deutscher Automobil-Club (ADAC), FIA & AIT, Am Westpark 8, 81373 München. ☎ (089) 76760. 24-hour information service, ☎ (089) 22222. Office hours: weekdays 0800-1700, Sat ADAC District Offices in main towns open 0800-1200.
Automobil-Club von Deutschland (AVD), *FIA*, Lyonerstrasse 16, 60528 Frankfurt-am-Main. ☎ (069) 6606-0. Office hours: weekdays 0800-1700.

Accidents and emergencies
Police ☎ 110, Fire Brigade ☎ 112, Ambulance ☎ 110.

Breakdowns
Both the motoring clubs (above) maintain emergency patrol services on motorways and main routes.

Carriage of children
Children under 12 are not permitted in front seats unless a seat equipped with a child restraint is fitted. In the rear of a vehicle, children under 12 must use a child seat, if fitted (a fine of 40 DM can be imposed if this regulation is not observed).

Crash helmets
Compulsory for motorcyclists and passengers.

Drinking and driving
The blood alcohol legal limit is 80mg.

Drivers
The minimum age for drivers is 17.

Driving licence
UK driving licence accepted.

Fuel
Leaded petrol: Super (98 octane) available. *Unleaded petrol*: Regular (91 octane) and Super (95/98 octane) available; pump legend *bleifrei normal or bleifrei super*. *Credit cards*: accepted at most petrol stations. *Spare fuel*: a full can of fuel may be imported duty free for use by vehicles registered in an EU country.

Lighting
When visibility is reduced by rain, fog or snow, use dipped headlights – driving with sidelights only is prohibited. Auxiliary/foglights should be used only with dipped headlights, even in daylight. Motorcyclists are advised to use headlights at all times.

Motorways
There are no tolls payable on autobahns. Fuel, restaurant and accommodation facilities, usually open 24 hours, are widely available on the network.

Overtaking
Do not overtake when passengers are boarding or

alighting from a bus or tram. Do not overtake a tram if there is insufficient room on the right. In one-way streets trams can be overtaken on either side, but normally on the right when in motion. You must indicate your intention when overtaking or changing lanes. In urban areas there is free choice of traffic lane if several lanes are available. It is prohibited to overtake or pass a school bus, which has stopped outside a built-up area, when red lights are flashing.

Parking
Except for one-way streets, parking is only permitted on the right side unless loading, boarding, or unloading. Do not park on roads with priority road signs, or where it would be dangerous to other traffic or pedestrians, outside built-up areas. Both meters and parking disc zones are in use.

Pedestrian crossings
Do give a pedestrian absolute priority on all pedestrian crossings, which are indicated on the road by white bands 50cm wide.

Priority
At the junction of two main roads or two minor roads, traffic from the right has priority, unless the contrary is indicated. Main road traffic has priority and that travelling on motorways has priority over vehicles entering or leaving.

Vehicles turning left at an intersection must give way to all oncoming vehicles. Trams do not have priority; buses do have priority when leaving bus stops. You must give way to a bus driver who has signalled his intention to leave the kerb.

Road signs
Most conform to the international pattern. Other road signs which may be seen are:
Autobahn kreuz: motorway junction
Baustofflagerung: roadworks material
Einbahnstrasse: one-way street
Fahrbahnwechsel: change traffic lane
Frostschäden: frost damage
Glatteisgefahr: ice on the road
Radweg kreuzt: cycle track crossing
Rollsplitt: loose grit
Seitenstreifen nicht bafahrbar: use of verge not advised
STAU: slow-moving traffic – drive with care
Strassenschäden: road damage
Umleitung: diversion

Seat belts
If fitted, compulsory use in front and rear seats.

Signalling
Do not sound your horn unnecessarily; this is forbidden. Outside built-up areas audible warning may be given if the driver intends to overtake another vehicle. At night, drivers must give warning of their approach by flashing their headlights.

Speed limits
Built-up areas: 31mph (50kmh); *outside built-up areas*: 62-81mph (100-130kmh); on *motorways*, the recommended maximum is 81mph (130kmh). These speed limits also apply in the five federal states, formerly East Germany. Cars towing a caravan or trailer are limited to 50mph (80kmh) on all roads outside built-up areas.

There is a minimum speed of 37mph (60kmh) on motorways and expressways. When visibility is below 50 metres, the maximum speed limit is 31mph (50kmh) on all roads.

Traffic lights
The international three colour system is used throughout Germany. A red light with a green filter arrow pointing to the right permits a right turn, however, motorists must give way to other road users and pedestrians.

Traffic offences
The German police are empowered to impose and collect on-the-spot fines of up to 75 DM. Motorists may pay the fine during the course of the following week. In cases of speed limit violations, a sliding scale of fines operates. A visitor can be asked to deposit a sum of money, and if he refuses or cannot pay, the vehicle may be impounded.

Warning triangle
Compulsory.

GENERAL INFORMATION
Banks
Open Mon-Fri 0830-1230 and 1330-1430 (Thu 1730). Closed Sat.
Currency
Deutschmark.
Public holidays
New Year's Day; Good Friday; Easter Monday; Labour Day; Ascension; Whit Monday; Day of Unity, 17 June; Unification Day, 3 Oct; Christmas, 25, 26 Dec. In addition, some areas observe Epiphany, Corpus Christi, Assumption, All Saints and Repentance days.
Shops
Open Mon-Fri 0830/0900-1800/1830. Close Sat at 1400.
To make a BT Chargecard call to the UK
Dial the BT Direct number 0130 80 0044 to contact a BT operator in the UK who will connect the call.

GIBRALTAR GBZ

MOTORING INFORMATION
RAC Agent A M Capurro and Sons Ltd, 20 Line Wall Road, Gibraltar. ☎ 75149.

Caravans and camping
The temporary importation of trailer caravans and motor caravans is prohibited, although Customs may grant an exception provided the owner is a bona fide visitor and does not intend to use the vehicle for camping purposes.

Crash helmets
Compulsory for motorcyclists and passengers on machines over 50cc.

Driving licence
UK driving licence accepted.

Accidents and emergencies
Police ☎ 190, Fire Brigade and Ambulance ☎ 199.

Fuel
Leaded petrol: Super (98 octane) available. Unleaded petrol: Super (95 octane) available. *Credit cards*: not accepted. *Spare fuel*: 20 gallons may be imported in a sealed steel container. It must be declared to Customs, and duty is payable.

Lighting
You must drive with dipped headlights at night.

Parking
Car parks are at Grand Parade (near lower cable car station), at Eastern Beach, Catalan Bay and at Casemates Square. Street parking is allowed in Queensway, Line Wall Road, Devils Tower Road and Rosia Road. Much of the town centre is pedestrianised, so motorists should park outside the city walls. Vehicles parked in restricted areas will be towed away or immobilised. If this occurs the driver should go to the Central Police Station in Irish Town. Parking areas are clearly marked.

Priority
Vehicles already on a roundabout have priority.

Roads
On the Upper Rock, roads are narrow, winding and steep. Signposts indicate those roads not open to civilian traffic. Visitors are therefore recommended to take a Rock Tour by taxi or minicoach.

Seat belts
Recommended.

Speed limits
Maximum 25mph (40kmh). Lower limits are signposted.

GENERAL INFORMATION
Banks
Open Mon-Thu 0900-1530 (Fri some open 0900-1800).

Border crossing
Motorists should beware of civilians illegally selling tickets for the border crossing.

Public holidays
New Year's Day; Commonwealth Day, 13 Mar; Easter; May Day; Spring Bank Holiday; Queen's Birthday; Late Summer Bank Holiday; Christmas.

Shops
Open Mon-Fri 0900-1700, Sat 0900-1300.

To make a BT Chargecard call to the UK
Dial the BT Direct number 84 00 to contact a BT operator in the UK who will connect the call.

GREECE GR

MOTORING INFORMATION
National motoring organisations
The Automobile and Touring Club of Greece (ELPA), *FIA & AIT*, 2-4 Messogion Street (Athens Tower), 115 27 Athí na (Athens). ☎ 748 8800. Office hours: Mon-Fri 0830-1930, Sat 0830-1330.

Accidents and emergencies
Police ☎ 100 (Athí na, Pireás, Thessaloní ki, Pátrai, Corfu), 109 (suburbs of Athí na); Fire Brigade ☎ 199, Ambulance ☎ 166 (Athí na) – for other towns see local directory.

Breakdowns
ELPA's road assistance service (OVELPA) operates on a 24-hour basis and covers all main roads, as well as the islands of Crete and Corfu. For assistance ☎ 104.

Carriage of children
It is prohibited for children under the age of 10 to travel in the front seat.

Crash helmets
Compulsory for motorcyclists and passengers.

Drinking and driving
The blood alcohol legal limit is 50mg.

Drivers
The minimum age for drivers is 18.

Driving licence
UK driving licence accepted.

Fire extinguisher
Compulsory.

First aid kit
Compulsory.

Fuel

Leaded petrol: Regular (91/92 octane) and Super (98 octane) available. *Unleaded petrol*: Super (95/98 octane) available; pump legend *amoliwdi wensina*. *Credit cards*: accepted at some petrol stations. *Spare fuel*: it is prohibited to import fuel in cans.

Lighting

Do not use undipped headlights in towns. A motor vehicle parked at night on a public road must have the rear red light clearly illuminated.

Overtaking

Overtaking is prohibited when approaching an unguarded level crossing.

Parking

The usual restrictions apply. Some streets have only unilateral parking, or impose a 30-minute limit. In Athína you may park only at meters although special parking sites are available to visitors. Caravans are also admitted for parking. The police will remove your registration plates if you stop or park in a no-parking zone. This practice applies also in some areas outside Athína. Greek-registered vehicles have been banned from a zone in the centre of Athína on certain days. Visiting motorists are exempted if their stay in Greece does not exceed 40 days.

Priority

In towns priority must be accorded to traffic entering from the right. In the open country, main road traffic has priority.

Road signs

International road signs are in use.

Seat belts

If fitted, compulsory use in front seats.

Signalling

Your warning device must be of low-pitched regular tone. Multitone sirens, klaxons, whistles and hooters are forbidden. The horn may be used in open country, but in towns it is allowed only in an emergency.

Speed limits

Built-up areas: motorcycles 25mph (40kmh), car with or without caravan/trailer 31mph (50kmh). *Outside built-up areas*: motorcycles 44mph (70kmh), car with or without caravan/trailer 68mph (110kmh). *Motorways and national roads:* motorcycles 56mph (90kmh), car with or without caravan/trailer 75mph (120kmh) on motorways.

Tolls

Payable on certain roads (see page 75).

Traffic offences

Fines imposed by the Greek police are payable to the Public Treasury, not to a police officer.

Warning triangle

Compulsory.

GENERAL INFORMATION

Banks

Open Mon-Fri 0800-1800 in major tourist areas. Foreign exchange counters often open again in the afternoon and evening.

Currency

Drachma.

Public holidays

New Year's Day; Epiphany; Independence Day, 25 Mar; Shrove Monday; Good Friday; Easter Monday; Labour Day; Whit Monday; Assumption, 15 Aug; Ohi Day (National Day), 28 Oct; Christmas, 25, 26 Dec

Shops

Usually open Mon 0930-1900, Tue-Fri 0900-1900, Saturday 0900-1530.

To make a BT Chargecard call to the UK

Dial the BT Direct number 00 800 4411 to contact a BT operator in the UK who will connect the call. Available from all the Greek islands.

HUNGARY H

MOTORING INFORMATION

National motoring organisation

Magyar Autóklub (MAK), *FIA & AIT*, Rómer Flóris utca 4/a, Budapest II. ☎ 1-212 2938. Office hours: Mon-Thu 0730-1600, Fri 0730-1500. Closed Sat.

Accidents and emergencies

Police ☎ 07, Fire Brigade ☎ 05, Ambulance ☎ 04. An '0' prefix should be added when calling emergency services from outside Budapest. Accidents causing damage or injury to persons must be reported to the nearest policeman or police station (☎ Budapest 07) and to the Hungarian State Insurance Company within 24 hours. The police will issue a statement, which the motorist must show when leaving Hungary, in order to avoid lengthy delays at the frontier.

Carriage of children

Children under 12 or less than 150cm in height, are not allowed to travel on the front seat unless the vehicle has a child restraint seat.

Crash helmets
Compulsory for motorcyclists and passengers on machines over 50cc which can exceed 50kmh.
Drinking and driving
The blood alcohol legal limit is 0mg.
Drivers
The minimum age for drivers is 18.
Driving licence
EC format pink/green licence accepted; old-style green licence accepted only if accompanied by an International Driving Permit.
Fuel
On motorways and in large towns, petrol stations are open 24 hours. Otherwise, hours are 0600-2000. *Leaded petrol*: 98 octane available. *Unleaded petrol*: Regular (91 octane) and Super (95/98 octane) available; pump legend *olommentes uzemanyag*. Availability is indicated by a white sign with blue border and an illustration of two pumps – black (leaded) and green (unleaded). *Diesel*: visiting motorists are recommended to fill their tanks at SHELL or AFOR stations to avoid inferior fuel on sale at some filling stations. *Credit cards*: Eurocard accepted at some petrol stations. *Spare fuel*: it is prohibited to import or export fuel in cans. *Coupons*: the coupon scheme has been discontinued.
Lighting
Outside built-up areas, including motorways, dipped headlights must be used day and night. In built-up areas at night, the use of full headlights is prohibited, and dipped headlights must be used. Motorcyclists must use dipped headlights day and night. Additional stop lights are prohibited. A spare set of bulbs must be carried by residents only.
Motorways
Emergency telephones are located at 2km intervals on motorways. Catering facilities are usually located near petrol stations. Motel accommodation is rarely available on motorways.
Overtaking
Vehicles must overtake on the left. On roads where tram-rails are placed in the middle of the road, a moving tram or vehicle signalling its intention to turn left must be overtaken on the right.
Parking
To reduce traffic congestion and pollution, the centre of Budapest is closed to private traffic. On two-way roads vehicles must be parked on the right-hand side of the road, facing in the direction of the traffic. They may be parked on either side of one-way roads. Do not park in places where you would not park in Britain.
Pedestrian crossings
Pedestrians have right of way at pedestrian crossings and priority at intersections over turning traffic. They do not have priority on the roadway between tramloading islands and the kerb. Drivers must show special care on these sections.
Priority
Major roads are indicated by a priority road ahead sign. At the intersection of two roads of equal importance, where there is no such sign, vehicles coming from the right have priority. However, emergency vehicles, with a blue light or siren, and trams and buses have absolute priority at any intersection and, indeed, on any road.
Buses also have right of way when leaving bus stops after the driver has signalled his intention to pull out.
Road signs
utca: street
ter: square
korut: boulevard
Seat belts
If fitted, compulsory use in front and rear seats.
Signalling
The use of horns in built-up areas is not permitted between 2200 and 0600. During these hours, warning signals must be given by means of headlights. Motorists are also prohibited to use a horn at any time in Budapest and in certain other towns and villages on main roads, except in an emergency.
Speed limits
Built-up areas: motorcycles, cars with or without caravan/trailer 31mph (50kmh). *Outside built-up areas*: motorcycles, cars 50mph (80kmh), dual carriageways 62mph (100kmh), motorways 75mph (120kmh). Car with caravan/trailer on normal roads and dual carriageways 44mph (70kmh), on motorways 50mph (80kmh).
Tolls
See page 76
Traffic offences
On-the-spot fines up to 5000 HUF are imposed and collected by the police. *Credit cards* are not accepted. Alternatively, fines may be paid by post within 15 days.
Warning triangle
Compulsory.

GENERAL INFORMATION
Banks
Open Monday 0815-1800, Tues-Thurs 0815-1500,-Fri 0815-1300.
Currency
Forint. The official abbreviation of the forint is HUF, but the old abbreviation Ft. is still used. Visitors must be in possession of the equivalent of 5,000 HUF in hard currency. Exemptions from this regulation are visitors holding credit card, letter of invitation or accommodation vouchers issued by a travel agency.

Museums
Open Tue-Sat 1000-1800.
Public holidays
New Year; 15 Mar; Easter Monday; Whitsun; Labour Day;
Constitution Day, 20 Aug; Proclamation of the Republic,
23 Oct; Christmas, 25, 26 Dec.
Shops
Open Mon-Fri 1000-1800, Sat 1000-1300.

To make a BT Chargecard call to the UK
Dial the BT Direct number 09 (Budapest) or 01 (rest of
country) to contact a BT operator in the UK who will
connect the call. Available from all phones.
Visa
British Nationals no longer require a visa.

REPUBLIC OF IRELAND

IRL

MOTORING INFORMATION
Accidents and emergencies
Police, Fire, Ambulance ☎ 999.
Carriage of children
Not permitted under 12 in front seat, unless the seat is
equipped with a child restraint.
Crash helmets
Compulsory for motorcyclists and passengers.
Drinking and driving
A person convicted of driving or attempting to drive
with a blood alcohol level exceeding 80mg will be liable
to a severe penalty.
Drivers
The minimum age for drivers is 17.
Driving licence
UK driving licence accepted.
Fuel
Petrol stations are usually open from 0730 to 2200, and
some are open 24 hours. *Leaded petrol*: Super
(98 octane) available. *Unleaded petrol*: widely available.
Credit cards: accepted. *Spare fuel*: although up to
10 litres may be imported duty free in containers, do
remember that it is illegal to carry spare fuel on ferries.
Internal ferries
A car ferry operates across the River Shannon from
Tarbert (Co. Kerry) to Killimer (Co. Clare). The ferry
leaves Killimer hourly on the hour, and Tarbert hourly
on the half-hour. Crossing time is 30 minutes.
A 10-minute car ferry service operates between
Ballyhack (Co. Wexford) and Passage East (Co.
Waterford). First sailing 0720 weekdays, 0930 Sunday.
Last sailing 2200 in summer, 2000 in winter.
Lighting
Foglights may only be used in fog or falling snow.
Parking
The usual restrictions apply as in Great Britain. Parking
meters are in use. They operate from Monday to
Saturday from 0800 to 1830 and the maximum
authorised parking time is 2 hours. Free use of
unexpired time on meters is authorised. On-the-spot
fines may be levied for parking offences.

Road signs
The 'Give Way' sign is a red triangle with the point
downwards, and words 'Yield Right of Way' or '*Geill sli*'.
Seat belts
If fitted, compulsory use in front and rear seats.
Signalling
Horns must not be used between 2330 and 0700 on any
road where a permanent speed limit is in force.
Speed limits
Built-up areas: 30mph (48kmh); *outside built-up
areas*: 60mph (96kmh); *motorways*: 70mph (112kmh).
On certain roads, and clearly marked, the speed limits
are 40mph (64kmh) or 50mph (80kmh). Cars towing a
trailer/caravan are limited to 50mph (80kmh) on all
roads.
Temporary importation of vehicles
Drivers of motor caravans, caravans and trailers will be
issued with a temporary importation permit by Irish
Customs at the port of arrival. A temporarily imported
vehicle must not be driven by an Irish resident.
Traffic offences
If a motorist has committed an offence the Garda
Siochana (Civic Guard) may issue the person with a
notice instructing the offender to pay a fine within
21 days at a Garda Station. The offender has an
alternative choice of letting the case go to court.

GENERAL INFORMATION
Banks
Open Mon-Fri 1000-1230 and 1330-1500 (in Dublin,
until 1700 on Thursdays).
Currency
Irish punt.
Museums
Generally open 1000-1700 daily except public holidays.
Passport
British citizens born in the United Kingdom do not
require a passport to visit Ireland.
Public holidays
New Year's Day; St Patrick's Day, 17 Mar; Easter; first
Mon in June and Aug; last Mon in Oct; Christmas.

Shops
Open Mon-Sat 0900-1730/1800.

ITALY (I)

MOTORING INFORMATION

National motoring organisations

Automobile Club d'Italia (ACI), *FIA & AIT*, Via
Marsala 8, 00185 Roma. ☎ (06) 4998 21. Office hours:
Mon-Sat 0800-1400 and 1500-1900. Offices in most large
towns.
Touring Club Italiano (TCI), *AIT*, Corso Italia 10,
20122 Milano. ☎ (02) 85261. Head Office hours: Mon-
Fri 0900-1800, Sat 0830-1230. For breakdown service
information, ☎ 8526263.

Accidents and emergencies
Police ☎ 113, Fire Brigade ☎ 115, Ambulance ☎ 118.

Breakdowns
In the case of breakdown, ☎ 116. This puts the traveller
in touch with the ACI breakdown service. Motoring
visitors can also use this number for urgent medical or
legal advice.

Carriage of children
Children aged between 4 and 12 must occupy a front or
rear seat which is equipped with a special restraint.

Car theft
To combat the major problem of car theft, the
authorities are increasing the number of spot checks of
foreign registered vehicles. Drivers must be able to
present vehicle documents, including authorisation
from the vehicle owner to use the vehicle, and personal
papers. Failure to do so can result in confiscation of the
vehicle.

Crash helmets
Compulsory for motorcyclists and passengers.

Drinking and driving
The blood alcohol legal limit is 80mg.

Drivers
The minimum age for drivers is 18.

Driving licence
EC format pink/green licence accepted; old-style green
licence accepted only with an official Italian translation
issued by consulate, alternatively, International Driving
Permit accepted.

Fuel
On motorways, petrol stations are open 24 hours. On
other roads, fuel is available (May to September) 0700-
1230, and 1530-1930. From October to April, petrol
stations close at 1900. Only 25% of petrol stations on
these roads are open on Sundays and public holidays,
and are subsequently closed on Mondays. Opening

hours are displayed, along with the address of the
nearest garage open. Fuel prices are increased by 20 lire
on motorways with a further 20 lire surcharge for night
service (not applicable at automatic pumps). *Leaded
petrol*: Super (98/100 octane) available. *Unleaded
petrol*: Super (95 octane) available; pump legend
benzina sensa piombo. *Credit cards*: accepted at
motorway service stations and at 70% of petrol stations
on ordinary roads. *Spare fuel*: it is prohibited to import
and carry fuel in cans. *Coupons*: the coupon scheme has
been discontinued.

Lighting
It is compulsory to use vehicle lights half an hour after
sunset until half an hour before sunrise. Main beam
headlights can only be used *outside* towns, and when
no other vehicle is approaching. At all other times, only
low beam headlights can be used. Lights must be used
under bridges and dipped lights must be used in
tunnels. Foglights should only be used in bad visibility.

Overhanging load
An overhanging load (e.g. bicycle carried behind car or
caravan) must be indicated by a square panel 50cm by
50cm with reflectorised red and white diagonal stripes.
The sign is available from motor caravan/caravan
dealerships in the UK. A fine of 100,000 lire may be
imposed if the sign is not displayed.

Overtaking
You may overtake on the right when the other driver
has signalled he is turning left and has moved to the
centre of the road, or when travel is in parallel lanes.

Parking
This is allowed on the right side of the road, except on
motorways (*autostrada*) and in places where you
would not park in Britain.
There are Blue Zones in all major towns, indicated by
road signs. Within these zones a parking disc must be
displayed from Monday to Saturday (except holidays)
0900-1430 and 1600-2000. The maximum period is one
hour. Discs are obtained from the tourist and
automobile organisations and petrol stations. There are
also Green Zones where parking is strictly prohibited on
weekdays 0800-0930 and 1430-1600.
Vénezia Owing to the limited parking facilities at the
Venezia end of the causeway, especially in the Piazzale
Roma, it is advisable to park at one of the special car
parks on the mainland. The car parks are linked by ferry

and bus services to destinations in Venezia.
Roma Parking is strictly prohibited in the central area on weekdays, indicated by a sign reading *zona tutelato*. Illegal parking will result in a fine and a prison sentence.
Firenze (Florence) Vehicles are banned from the centre on weekdays 0730-1830. Visitors staying within the area may stop to offload luggage, but then must park outside the restricted area.

Priority
On three-lane roads, the middle lane is reserved for overtaking. At crossroads, give way to traffic from the right. Outside built-up areas priority must be given to vehicles travelling on national roads (*strade statali*). On certain mountain roads, a red circular sign bearing a black post horn on a white triangle indicates that vehicles are required to stop at the approach of buses belonging to the postal services.

Road signs
Most conform to the international pattern. Other road signs which may be encountered are:
Entrata: entrance
Incrocio: crossroads
Lavori in corso: roadworks ahead
Passaggio a livello: level crossing
Rallentare: slow down
Senso Vietato: no entry
Sosta Autorizzata: parking permitted (followed by indication of times)
Sosta Vietata: no parking
Svolta: bend
Uscita: exit
Vietato Ingresso Veicoli: no entry for vehicles
Vietato Transito Autocarri: closed to heavy vehicles

Seat belts
If fitted, compulsory use in front and rear seats.

Signalling
In built-up areas use of the horn is prohibited except in cases of immediate danger. At night, flashing headlights may be used instead of a horn. Outside built-up areas, when it is required that warning of approach be given, the use of the horn is compulsory.

Speed limits
Built-up areas : all vehicles 30mph (50kmh). *Outside built-up areas*, motorcycles over 150cc and cars; on secondary roads 55mph (90kmh), main roads 68mph (110kmh), *motorways*: 80mph (130kmh).
Motorcaravans between 3.5 and 12 tonnes : *outside* built up areas 50mph (80kmh), motorways 62mph (100kmh). Motorcaravans over 12 tonnes and car towing a caravan or trailer are limited to 44mph

(70kmh) outside built up areas and 50mph (80kmh) on motorways.

Tolls
Tolls are payable on the autostrada network (see page 76). Credit cards are accepted for payment on the A4, A22, A28 and A32 motorways only. On most motorways (except Sicily) motorists may pay for tolls with a magnetic card called a VIACARD. The card is available in varying denominations from toll booths, service areas, certain banks and tourist offices. The card is valid until expiry of credit and can be used on subsequent visits.

Traffic offences
The police can impose a fine on the driver of a foreign registered vehicle and collect one quarter of the maximum fine on the spot. If the driver wishes to contest the fine or refuses to pay, a guarantee for half the maximum amount must be deposited, either in cash (foreign currency accepted) or in the form of a surety. If the guarantee is not deposited, the driving licence may be withdrawn. If the licence is not available, the car may be confiscated until the fine is paid.

Warning triangle
Compulsory.

GENERAL INFORMATION
Banks
Open Mon-Fri 0830-1330 and 1500-1600.
Currency
Lire.
Public holidays
New Year's Day; Easter Monday; Liberation Day, 25 Apr; Labour Day; Assumption, 15 Aug; All Saints Day, 1 Nov; Immaculate Conception, 8 Dec; Christmas, 25, 26 Dec. It is wise to check locally for shop and bank closing times on special Feast days.
Purchase of meals
Visitors to Italy should obtain a specially numbered receipt (*Ricevuta fiscale*) when paying for a meal in restaurants, hotels, etc. This fiscal receipt must show the amount paid for each part of the meal and the VAT paid. Visitors must ensure that this receipt is issued, as a fine may be imposed for non-compliance.
Shops
Open Mon-Sat 0830/0900-1300 and 1530/1600-1930/2000 with some variations in the north, where the lunch break is shorter and shops close earlier.
To make a BT Chargecard call to the UK
Dial the BT Direct number 15 to contact a BT operator in the UK who will connect the call. Payphones require Gettoni or 200 Lira coin to access 15, which is returned.

LUXEMBOURG   L

MOTORING INFORMATION
National motoring organisation
Automobile Club du Grand Duché de Luxembourg (ACL), *FIA & AIT*, 54 route de Longwy, 8007 Bertrange. ☎ 450045-1. Office hours: Mon-Fri 0830-1200 and 1330-1800.
Accidents and emergencies
Police ☎ 113, Fire Brigade and Ambulance ☎ 012.
Carriage of children
A child under 12, or below 1.5 metres in height, may only occupy a front seat in a special safety-approved seat. In the rear, a child should be seated in a child seat, or use a seat belt.
Crash helmets
Compulsory for motorcyclists and passengers.
Drinking and driving
The blood alcohol legal limit is 80mg.
Drivers
The minimum age for drivers is 18.
Driving licence
UK driving licence accepted.
Fuel
Leaded petrol: Super (98 octane) available. *Unleaded petrol*: Super (95 octane) available; pump legend *essence sans plomb*. *Credit cards*: Visa and Eurocard accepted. *Spare fuel*: it is prohibited to purchase and carry spare fuel in cans.
Lighting
Use dipped headlights when visibility is reduced due to fog, heavy rain or snow during daylight hours. It is compulsory to use dipped headlights in built-up areas. In other places vehicles must have dipped or undipped headlights. Motorcyclists must use dipped headlights day and night.
Overtaking
Avoid when this might endanger or obstruct traffic.
Parking
A Blue Zone parking area exists in Luxembourg City, Esch-sur-Alzette, Dudelange and Wiltz. Parking discs follow the usual pattern and are obtainable from the ACL, police stations, local tourist office, shops, etc. Luxembourg City has coin parking meters and ticket parking tickets obtainable at dispensing boxes. Illegally parked vehicles will be clamped by the police.

Priority
The rule of the road is keep to the right, overtake on the left. At a crossing of two roads in the same category, traffic from the right has priority. In towns, do give priority to traffic coming from the right, unless the crossing is marked with a triangular sign.
Seat belts
If fitted, compulsory use in front and rear seats.
Signalling
Unnecessary use of the horn is prohibited. Do not use it between nightfall and dawn, or in built-up areas, except in an emergency. During the day, warning of approach should be given before overtaking another vehicle, or at places where visibility is restricted or whenever road safety requires it. At night, in these circumstances, it is compulsory to flash headlights.
Speed limits
Built-up areas: 30mph (50kmh); *outside built-up areas*: 56mph (90kmh); *motorways*: 74mph (120kmh). Cars towing a caravan or trailer are limited to 46mph (75kmh;) *outside built-up areas*, and 56mph (90kmh) on motorways.
Traffic offences
On-the-spot fines are imposed by police in cases of traffic offences.
Warning triangle
Compulsory.

GENERAL INFORMATION
Banks
Open Mon-Fri 0830-1200 and 1330-1630.
Currency
Luxembourg and Belgian francs.
Public holidays
New Year's Day; Carnival Day mid February*; Easter Monday; May Day; Ascension; Whit Monday; National Day, 23 June; Assumption, 15 Aug; All Saints; All Souls*; Christmas, 25, 26 Dec. (* although not an official holiday, banks and offices are closed and most shops are closed, particularly in the afternoon.)
Shops
Open Mon 1400-1830, Tue-Sat 0830-1200 and 1400-1830.
To make a BT Chargecard call to the UK
Dial the BT Direct number 0800 0044 to contact a BT operator in the UK who will connect the call. Available from Post Offices.

NETHERLANDS

MOTORING INFORMATION

National motoring organisations
Koninklijke Nederlandsche Automobiel Club (KNAC), *FIA*, Binckhorstlaan 115, Den Haag 2516 BA. ☎ (070) 383 1612. Office hours: Mon-Fri 0900-1700.
Koninklijke Nederlandsche Toeristenbond (ANWB), *AIT*, Wassenaarsweg 220, Den Haag. ☎ (070) 314 7147. Office hours: Mon-Fri 0800-1730.

Accidents and emergencies
Police, Fire Brigade and Ambulance, ☎ 06-11

Carriage of children
Children under three must travel in the rear with a safety system adapted to their size. Those aged three to 12 may travel in a front seat if in a special safety seat.

Crash helmets
Compulsory for motorcyclists and passengers.

Drinking and driving
The blood alcohol legal limit is 50mg.

Drivers
The minimum age for drivers is 18.

Driving licence
UK driving licence accepted.

Fuel
Leaded petrol: Super (98 octane) available. *Unleaded petrol*: Super (95 and 98 octane) available; pump legend *loodvrije benzine. Credit cards*: accepted. *Spare fuel*: 10 litres of petrol in a can may be imported duty free.

Internal ferries
A car ferry service operates across the Westerschelde estuary between Breskens and Vlissingen, and further east between Perkpolder and Kruiningen. Journey time is 20 mins and 15 mins respectively.

Lighting
Parked vehicles do not have to be illuminated at night, provided they are parked in a built-up area, within 30 metres of a street lighting point, or in an official car park. Inside built-up areas only dipped headlights (low beam) are permitted. Dipped or full headlights must be used in fog.

Overtaking
Do not cross a continuous white line on the road, even to make a left turn. You may overtake stationary trams on the right at moderate speed, provided no inconvenience is caused to persons entering or leaving the tram. The overtaking of moving trams is normally permitted only on the right, although if there is insufficient room and no danger to oncoming traffic, vehicles may overtake on the left. The 'overtaking prohibited' sign does not apply to scooters or solo motorcycles. Do follow correct lanes, these are well marked with arrows.

Parking
Do not park on roads signposted 'No Parking', in front of driveways or where you may obscure road, street or traffic signs; on priority roads outside built-up areas. Do not halt a vehicle on roads signposted *Stop-verbod* – a blue disc with a red border and red diagonals; on access roads to and from main highways; cycling paths or footpaths, or along a yellow line or black and white line painted on road or pavement alongside a bus stop; in the middle of a three-lane road, or on a road with more than three lanes (this does not stop passengers getting in or out of a car); on level crossings. Blue Zones have been introduced in most towns and free parking discs are obtainable from police stations. A parking fee is charged at guarded car parks. There are also parking meters. Wheel clamps will be used on illegally parked vehicles.

Priority
Priority roads are indicated by diamond-shaped yellow signs with white borders. At junctions where the sign 'major road ahead' or 'stop, major road ahead' is displayed, priority must be given to all traffic on that road. At the intersection of two roads of the same class where there are no signs, traffic from the right has preference. Motor vehicles have right of way over slow traffic, such as bicycles. Ambulances, fire engines, police cars and emergency rescue vehicles always have right of way. Trams have priority at intersections of equal importance but they must yield right of way to traffic on priority roads. At intersections, cyclists proceeding straight ahead have priority over all traffic. At pedestrian crossings do give a pedestrian absolute priority if he is on the zebra crossing first.

Road signs
Most conform to the international pattern but other road signs which may be seen are :
Doorgaand verkeer gestremd: no throughway
Langzaam rijden: slow down
Opspattend Grind: loose grit
Pas op: filevorming: attention: single or double lane traffic ahead
Rechtsaf toegeslaan: right turn allowed
Tegenliggers: traffic from the opposite direction
Wegomlegging: detour
Werk in uitvoering: road building in progress
Watch for a blue sign with a white house emblem –
Woonerf: built-up area. This can mean:
1. Drive at walking pace (children playing in street);
2. Pedestrians have right of way;
3. Bicycles from the right have priority;
4. Park only in zones marked 'P'.

Seat belts
If fitted, compulsory use in front seats.
Signalling
Sound your horn where there is any risk to other road users. At night you should give warning by flashing headlights instead, unless this might cause interference to other traffic, in which case the horn may be used.
Speed limits
Built-up areas: 31mph (50kmh); *outside built-up areas*: 50mph (80kmh); *motorways*: 62-74mph (100-120kmh). The minimum speed on motorways is 37mph (60kmh). Cars towing a caravan or trailer with one axle, 50mph (80kmh) outside built-up areas.
Traffic offences
In some districts, on-the-spot fines are imposed and collected by the police.
Warning triangle
Compulsory.

GENERAL INFORMATION
Banks
Open Mon-Fri 0900-1600. At border towns, exchange offices (GWK) are open Mon-Sat, also often Sun and in the evenings.

Bicycles
Visitors should be prepared for heavy cycle traffic, particularly at peak hours. Cycle lanes marked by continuous white lines are prohibited to vehicles. Cycle lanes marked by a broken white line may be used by motor vehicles if they do not obstruct cyclists.
Currency
Guilder (florin).
Museums
Open Tue-Fri 1000-1700, Sat & Sun 1100-1700, or 1300-1700.
Public holidays
New Year's Day; Good Friday; Easter Monday; Queen's Birthday, 30 Apr; Liberation Day, 5 May; Ascension; Whit Monday; Christmas, 25, 26 Dec.
Shops
Department stores open Mon-Fri 0830/0900-1730/1800, Sat 0830/0900-1600/1700. Food shops open Mon-Sat 0800-1800. All traders are required by law to close their shops for one half day per week. Local regulations stipulate when all shops will be closed either until 1300, or from 1300 onwards.
To make a BT Chargecard call to the UK
Dial the BT Direct number 06 0410 to contact a BT operator in the UK who will connect the call.

NORWAY   N

MOTORING INFORMATION
National motoring organisations
Kongelig Norsk Automobilklub (KNA), *FIA,*
Drammensveien 20-C, 0255 Oslo. ☎ (47) 22-56 19 00. Office hours: Mon-Fri 0830-1600 (1500 in summer).
Norges Automobil-Forbund (NAF), *AIT,* Storgt. 2, 0155 Oslo 1. ☎ (47) 22-34 15 00. Telex: 71671. Office hours: Mon-Fri 0830-1600, Sat 0830-1300.
Accidents and emergencies
Police ☎ 112, Fire Brigade 110, Ambulance ☎ 113.
Breakdowns
During the summer season road patrols are maintained on most mountain passes and on certain main roads.
Carriage of children
Children under 4 years of age must be in a special restraint system. Children over 4 years of age must use a child restraint or a seat belt.
Crash helmets
Compulsory for motorcyclists and passengers.
Drinking and driving
The blood alcohol legal limit is 50mg.
Drivers
The minimum age for drivers is 17, or 18 to hire or borrow a locally registered vehicle.

Driving licence
UK driving licence accepted.
Fuel
Petrol stations are generally open between 0700 and 2200 hours. Some petrol stations remain open 24 hours a day in cities. *Leaded petrol*: Super (98 octane) available. *Unleaded petrol*: Super (95 octane) available; pump legend *blyfritt kraftstoff*. *Credit cards*: major cards accepted at larger petrol stations. *Spare fuel*: no more than 15 litres are recommended to carry in approved storage cans, which may be imported duty free.
Internal car ferries
Full details of car ferry services within Norway are given in a special timetable, available from the Norwegian Tourist Board annually in March on receipt of a large SAE with 50 pence postage.
Lighting
It is compulsory to use dipped headlights at all times. Foglights are not compulsory, but if used must be in conjunction with other lights. They may be used in fog or falling snow and in clear weather on winding roads.
Mountain passes
Many of the high mountain roads are closed during the winter, duration of closure depending on weather

conditions. However, some mountain passes are kept open all year, eg Road No. 11 (Oslo-Bergen/Stavanger) across Haukelifjell mountain, the E6 (Oslo-Trondheim) across Dovrefjell mountain, and Road No. 7 (Oslo-Bergen) over the Hardangervidda plateau.

Overtaking
In Oslo, normally overtake trams on the right: they may be overtaken on the left if in motion in a one-way street, or where there is no room on the right.

Parking
Do not park on main roads; where visibility is restricted; where there is a sign *All Stans Forbudt* (No stopping allowed), or you may have your car towed away. Parking regulations in Norwegian towns are very strict, and parking offences are invariably subject to fines. Parking meters are in use in the main towns. Free use of unexpired time on meters is authorised. There are three types of parking meter: Yellow – 1 hour parking, Grey – 2 hours, and Brown – 3 hours.

Priority
Give way to traffic from the right, except on some main roads which are given permanent priority. Intersecting junctions will bear the international priority symbol. Vehicles climbing uphill must be given priority, and down-hill drivers must reverse into a parking bay if necessary. Traffic on roundabouts has priority. Trams always have right of way.

Road signs
International road signs, but other road signs which may be seen are:
Arbeide pa Vegen: roadworks ahead
Bakketopp: hill top
Enveiskjøring: one-way traffic
Ferist: cattle grid
Gammel Veg: old road
Grøfterens: ditching work
Ikke Møte: no passing, single line traffic
Kjør Sakte: drive slowly
Løs Grus: loose gravel
Moteplass: passing bay
Omkjøring: diversion
Rasteplass: lay-by

Svake Kanter: soft verges
Veg under Anlegg: road under construction
Veiarbeide: roadworks

Seat belts
If fitted, compulsory use in front and rear seats. On-the-spot fines are imposed for non-compliance.

Signalling
Use horns, traffic indicators and lights only when necessary to avoid accidents.

Speed limits
Built-up areas: 31mph (50kmh); *outside built-up areas and on motorways*: 50-56mph (80-90kmh). Outside built-up areas, cars towing a caravan or trailer (with brakes) 50mph (80kmh); (without brakes) 37mph (60kmh).

Tolls
All vehicles entering Bergen by road on a weekday must pay a toll of 5 Kr. No charge at weekends or on public holidays. Cars or vehicles up to 3.5 tonnes entering Oslo pay a toll of 12 Kr and a toll of 10 Kr to enter Trondheim.

Traffic offences
Police are empowered to impose and collect fines on the spot in cases of traffic offences.

Warning triangle
Advisable.

GENERAL INFORMATION
Banks
Open Mon-Fri 0815-1500 (1530 in winter). Some banks open until 1700 on Thursdays.

Currency
Krone (plural kroner).

Public holidays
New Year's Day; Maundy Thursday; Good Friday; Easter Monday; Labour Day; Constitution Day, 17 May; Whit Monday; Ascension Day; Christmas, 24 (part), 25 and 26 Dec.

Shops
Open Mon/Wed/Fri 0900-1700, Thu 0900-1800, Sat 0900-1300. In July some shops close at 1500.

To make a BT Chargecard call to the UK
Dial the BT Direct number 800 19 044 to contact a BT operator in the UK who will connect the call.

POLAND ⬭ PL

MOTORING INFORMATION
National motoring organisations
Polski Zwiazek Motorowy (PZM), *FIA & AIT*, 66 Kazimierzowska Street, PL-02-518 Warszawa. ☎ (48) 22 499 361, 22 499 212. Touring office: Autotour s.r.l., 85 Solec Street, 00-950 Warszawa. ☎ (48) 22 498 449. Head Office hours: Mon-Fri 0745-1545; PZM Touring office hours: Mon-Fri 0800-1600.

Auto Assistance, 19 Sandomierska Street, 00-950 Warszawa. ☎ (48) 22-290 374.

Accidents and emergencies
Police ☎ 997, Fire Brigade ☎ 998, Ambulance ☎ 999. If you are involved in an accident you must report it to the nearest police station and Insurance Association. It is an offence not to render first aid to accident victims or to leave the scene of an accident.

Breakdowns
The Polski Zwiazek Motorway operates a road patrol service within a 25km radius of towns with a PZM office. Details are obtained from PZM frontier offices and provincial touring offices. In most towns, for breakdown assistance ☎ 981. Technical help is free to motorists belonging to AIT and FIA Clubs for repairs within the 25km area, which can be effected within an hour. For serious breakdowns the vehicle will be towed to a garage.

Carriage of children
A child up to 10 may only travel in the front if seated in a child seat.

Crash helmets
Compulsory for motorcyclists and passengers.

Drinking and driving
The blood alcohol legal limit is 20mg.

Drivers
The minimum age for drivers is 18.

Driving licence
Holders of green style licences require an International Driving Permit. Pink EC format licences are generally accepted by police authorities.

Fuel
Petrol stations generally open 0800-1900. In large towns, some stations open 24 hours. *Leaded petrol*: Regular (86 octane) and Super (94/98 octane) available. *Unleaded petrol*: Regular (82.5 octane) and Super (91 octane) available; pump legend *benzyna bezolowiu*. *Diesel*: available. *Spare fuel*: up to 10 litres of fuel may be imported and exported.

Lighting
At night in built-up areas, where street lighting is insufficient, drivers must use dipped headlights. During bad visibility, drivers must use passing lights and/or foglights. Use of front foglights is permitted on winding roads at night. Motorcyclists must use headlights at all times outside built-up areas. Between 1 November and 1 March, it is compulsory for all vehicles to use dipped headlights at all times.

Overtaking
The usual restrictions apply. Trams may be overtaken on the right. At tram stops without pedestrian islands, motorists should stop to let passengers walk between tram and pavement. During bad visibility drivers must give short audible warning signals before overtaking.

Parking
Parking is prohibited on certain streets signposted to that effect. On unlit streets, parking lights are obligatory during the hours of darkness.

Priority
In general, priority is given to vehicles coming from the right, but vehicles on major roads and roundabouts have right of way. Overtake trams on the right.

Road signs
International road signs.

Seat belts
If fitted, compulsory use in front and rear seats.

Signalling
Do not sound your horn in built-up areas. Some localities display signs prohibiting the use of horns in particular areas. Warning of approach should be given by flashing headlights and by short horn signals when driving in fog.

Speed limits
Built-up areas: 37mph (60kmh); *outside built-up areas*: 56mph (90kmh); *motorways*: 68mph (110kmh). The minimum speed on motorways is 24mph (40kmh). Cars towing a caravan or trailer, 44mph (70kmh) outside built-up areas, including motorways. In addition to built-up areas there are *residential zones*, indicated by 'entry/exit' signs, where the maximum speed permitted is 12mph (20kmh).

Traffic offences
Motorists who infringe traffic regulations may receive a verbal or written warning, or an on-the-spot fine of between 25,000 and 500,000 zlotys. A receipt must be provided by the police officer.

Warning triangle
Compulsory.

GENERAL INFORMATION

Banks
Usually open Mon-Fri 0800-1800, Sat (variable) 0800-1300/1700.

Currency
Zloty. Currency control regulations have been lifted and as a result the compulsory daily exchange procedure has been abolished, as have accommodation vouchers. Import and export of zlotys is prohibited. Foreign currency can be exchanged at frontier posts; branches of the Narodowy Bank Polski; the Bank of Commerce in Warszawa; hotel exchange offices, travel agencies and PZM frontier offices. It is essential to keep the conversion slips issued when currency is exchanged.

Public holidays
New Year's Day; Easter Monday; Labour Day; Constitution Day, 3 May; Corpus Christi; Feast of the Assumption, 15 Aug; All Saints, 1 Nov; Independence Day, 11 Nov; Christmas, 25, 26 Dec.

Shops
Food shops open Mon-Fri 0600-1900, Sat 0700-1300. Other shops open Mon-Fri 1100-2000, Sat 0900-1600.

To make a BT Chargecard call to the UK
Dial the BT Direct number 00 44 0099 48 to contact a BT operator in the UK who will connect the call. You can make international calls from all phones in Warsaw.

Visa
No longer required by British nationals.

PORTUGAL

MOTORING INFORMATION

National motoring organisation

Automóvel Club de Portugal (ACP), *FIA & AIT*, Rua Rosa Araújo 24, 1200 Lisboa. ☎ 1-356 39 31. Office hours: Mon-Fri 0900-1300 and 1400-1645. Touring reception: (Apr-Sep) Mon-Fri 0900-1730; (Oct-Mar) 0900-1645.

Accidents and emergencies

Police, Fire Brigade and Ambulance ☎ 115.

Breakdowns

For ACP breakdown service south of Pombal, ☎ Lisboa 942 50 95 and to the north, ☎ Porto 830 11 27.

Carriage of children

Not permitted under the age of 12 in the front seat, unless a child safety seat is fitted.

Crash helmets

Compulsory for motorcyclists and passengers.

Drinking and driving

The blood alcohol legal limit is 50mg.

Drivers

The minimum age for drivers is 17.

Driving licence

Old style green licences accepted if accompanied by an International Driving Permit.

Fuel

Petrol stations are open 0700-2200, 0700-2400, or 24 hours. *Leaded petrol*: Super (98 octane) available. *Unleaded petrol*: Super (95/98 octane) available; pump legend *gasolina sin plomo*. *Credit cards*: accepted. Purchase of fuel with a credit card incurs a surcharge of 100 Esc. *Spare fuel*: it is permitted to carry spare fuel.

Internal ferries

A car ferry service, operated by the Transado company, crosses the Sado estuary between Setúbal and Troia. There are 10 crossings per day between midnight and 2300, journey time 15 minutes. Services also operate from Lisboa across the Tagus (Tejo) estuary to Cacilhas, Barreiro, Montijo and Porto Brandão.

Lighting

In built-up areas, use dipped headlights at night.

Overtaking

The overtaking of stationary trams is permitted only if there is an island for embarking or disembarking passengers.

Parking

Parked vehicles must face in the same direction as moving traffic, except where parking is officially allowed on one side of the road only. Parking meters are in use in Lisbon, Oporto, Setubal, Albufeira, etc. Illegally parked vehicles will be immobilised and released only upon payment of a fine.

Priority

Do allow priority to traffic coming from the right.

Registration document

A special certificate, *Autorizacao*, will be required if the vehicle is not registered in your name – available from RAC Travel Information, ☎ 0345 333 222.

Roads

Roads are classified as follows: motorways (AE), principal roads (IP), national roads (EN), municipal roads (EM), other municipal roads (CM).

Seat belts

It is compulsory for all passengers to wear a seat belt, where fitted, at all times.

Signalling

Do not use the horn except to signal danger. Use flashing headlights at night and hand or mechanical indicators during the day.

Speed limits

Built-up areas: 31mph (50kmh); *outside built-up areas*: 56/62mph (90/100kmh); *motorways*: 74mph (120kmh). Cars towing a caravan or trailer are limited to 31mph (50kmh) in built-up areas, 43/50mph (70/80kmh) outside built-up areas, and 62mph (100kmh) on motorways. Minimum speed on motorways is 24mph (40kmh) unless otherwise indicated.

On the 25 de Abril Bridge, Lisboa, drivers must maintain a speed of 18-31mph (30-50kmh).

Visiting motorists who have held a full licence for under a year are limited to 56mph (90kmh), and a yellow disc showing the figure '90' must be displayed. Discs are available from ACP border offices.

Temporary importation of vehicles

It is recommended to obtain a tempoary importation form from a frontier customs office (Delegaçao Aduaneirá). This can be requested by police of foreign registered vehicles. An inventory of the contents of a caravan must be provided on plain paper or by filling in a form available at the frontier.

Tolls

Payable on certain roads (see page 77).

Traffic offences

The police are authorised to impose on-the-spot fines. A

receipt is issued to show that the fine has been paid. Fines are imposed for unauthorised parking, speeding, excess blood alcohol level, and failure to wear seat belts, if fitted. A motorist who refuses to pay the fine must pay a deposit to cover the maximum fine for the offence committed. If the deposit is not paid, the police will confiscate the vehicle.

Warning triangle
Compulsory.

GENERAL INFORMATION

Banks
Open Mon-Fri 0830-1445. Some large city banks operate a currency exchange service 1830-2300.

Currency
Escudos.

Museums
Open Tue-Sun 1000-1230 and 1400-1700.

Public holidays
New Year's Day; Carnival (Shrove Tuesday); Good Friday; Liberty Day, 25 Apr; Labour Day; Corpus Christi; Portugal Day, 10 June; St António, 13 June (Lisboa); São João, 24 June (Porto); Corpus Christi; Assumption, 15 Aug; Republic Day, 5 Oct; All Saints, 1 Nov; Independence Day, 1 Dec; Immaculate Conception, 8 Dec; Christmas, 24, 25 or 25, 26 Dec.

Shops
Open Mon-Fri 0900-1300 and 1500-1900, Sat 0900-1300. Shopping centres are open every day from 1000-2400.

To make a BT Chargecard call to the UK
Dial the BT Direct number 0505 00 44 to contact a BT operator in the UK who will connect the call.

Visitor Identification
All visitors should ensure identity documents eg passports are carried at all times when driving. Failure to do so will result in an on-the-spot fine.

ROMANIA   RO

MOTORING INFORMATION

National motoring organisation
Automobil Clubul Român (ACR), *FIA & AIT*, Str. Take Ionescu 27, 70154 Bucuresti 22. ☎ 8500 2595 (Touring Dept.). Office hours: Mon-Fri 0800-1600.

Accidents and emergencies
Police ☎ 955, Fire Brigade ☎ 981, Ambulance, ☎ 961. All accidents must be reported to the police. If the vehicle is damaged, a report must be obtained from the police to facilitate export of the vehicle from the country. A visitor in possession of a valid insurance policy will receive all assistance from CAROM (State Insurance Administration).

Breakdowns
For breakdown assistance please refer to European Motoring Assistance documentation.

Carriage of children
Children under the age of 12 are not permitted to travel on the front seat.

Crash helmets
Compulsory for motorcyclists and passengers.

Drinking and driving
Do not drink and drive: blood alcohol legal limit is 0mg.

Drivers
The minimum age for drivers is 18.

Driving licence
UK driving licence accepted.

Fuel
Leaded petrol: Super (96/98 octane) available. *Unleaded petrol*: Super (98 octane) widely available; pump legend *benzina fara plumb*. *Diesel*: available. *Spare fuel*: up to 10 litres of fuel in cans may be imported duty free. *Export of fuel*: A tax is levied on all petrol and diesel exported from Romania. *Coupons*: no longer required.

Lighting
In built-up areas, where roads are not lit, undipped headlights may be used for passing and at intersections. Where roads are lit, drivers must use dipped headlights only.

Overtaking
All vehicles must be overtaken on the left, except for trams which are overtaken on the right.

Parking
Stop or park vehicles on the right-hand side of the road in the direction of the traffic. Parking is prohibited on the carriageway of national highways.

Priority
At roundabouts, priority must be given to vehicles coming from the right. Vehicles already in the roundabout traffic must give way to vehicles entering the roundabout, as the latter come from the right.

Seat belts
Recommended.

Signalling
Use of the horn is prohibited in towns 2200-0600. At night, warning must be given by the use of lights. In Bucuresti and other towns, use of the horn is prohibited, and signs to this effect – *claxonarea interzisa* – warn motorists of this regulation.

Speed limits
Cars with or without caravan/trailer: *built-up areas* 37mph (60kmh); *outside built-up areas and on motorways*: under 1000cc, 44mph (70kmh), 1100-1800cc, 50mph (80kmh), over 1800cc 56mph (90kmh). *Motorcycles*: built-up areas 25mph (40kmh), outside built-up areas 37mph (60kmh).

Tolls
Charged for crossing the River Danube from Giurgiu to Ruse (Bulgaria), and from Giurgeni to Vadu Oii.

Traffic offences
Members of the Militia (police) may impose fines on the spot for violation of traffic regulations.

Warning triangle
Compulsory.

GENERAL INFORMATION
Banks
Open Mon-Fri 0900-1200, 1300-1500, Sat 0900-1230.
Currency
Leu (plural lei.)
Public holidays
New Year, 1, 2 Jan; International Labour Day, 1, 2 May; National Holiday, 23 24 Aug.
Shops
Open Mon-Fri 0800-2000, Sat 0800-2100. Sun 0800-1200.
To make a BT Chargecard call to the UK
Dial the BT Direct number 01 800 4444 to contact a BT operator in the UK who will connect the call. Available from all phones with access to long distance calls.
Visa
British Nationals must hold a valid passport and visa, available from: Romanian Consulate, 8 Palace Green, London W8, ☎ 0171-937 9667; or at the border and airports.

SLOVAKIA ⬭ SK

MOTORING INFORMATION
National motoring organisation
Ustredni Automotoklub SR, Wolkrova ul.c.4, 851 01 Bratislava. ☎ 7-85 09 11. Office hours Mon-Fri 0745-1645.

Accidents and emergencies
Police ☎ 158, Fire Brigade ☎ 150, Ambulance ☎ 155. If an accident causes bodily injury or material damage exceeding 1,000 SK, it must be reported to the police immediately. A certificate will be issued by the police to facilitate export of the vehicle. Accidents involving locally registered vehicles must be reported to the police and State Insurance Company.

Border crossing
All visitors must present their passports at the border between the Czech Republic and Slovakia.

Carriage of children
Children under 12, and persons under 4ft 9in (150cm), may not travel in front seats.

Drinking and driving
Do not drink and drive. No degree of alcohol in the blood is tolerated.

Drivers
The minimum age for drivers is 18.

Driving licence
UK driving licence accepted.

First aid kit
Compulsory.

Fuel
Petrol stations on international roads and in main towns are open 24 hours a day. *Leaded petrol*: Regular (90 octane) and Super (96 octane) available. *Unleaded petrol*: Super (95 octane) available; pump legend *Natural*. Maps showing outlets for unleaded petrol are issued at border crossings. *Diesel*: widely available. *Credit cards*: accepted by some petrol stations in main towns and tourist areas.

Lighting
Foglights may be used in case of fog, snow or heavy rain. If the vehicle is not equipped with foglights, the driver must use dipped headlights in these conditions. Motorcyclists must use dipped headlights at all times. At level crossings, waiting vehicles should emit sidelights only.

Overtaking
Overtaking regulations conform with international usage. Trams are overtaken on the right, unless there is no space, when it is permitted to overtake on the left. However in Bratislava, it is prohibited to overtake trams on the left and the driver must follow the tram until he has enough room to pass on the right. Drivers must not overtake near a tram refuge.

Parking
In a one-way street, parking is permitted on the left side only. Stopping and parking are prohibited in all places where visibility is poor or where the vehicle could cause an obstruction; in particular, near an intersection,

pedestrian crossing, bus or tram stop, level crossing and alongside a tram line unless there is still 3.5 metre wide side lane free. In Bratislava, parking is restricted in many places. Parking meters are being introduced in Bratislava and Kosice. Wheel clamps are also in use.

Priority
At uncontrolled crossroads or road intersections not marked by a priority sign, priority must be given to vehicles coming from the right. Drivers may not enter the intersection unless their exit is clear. A tram turning right and crossing the line of a vehicle on its right has priority once the driver has signalled his intention to turn.

Road signs
Most conform to the international pattern. Other road signs which may be seen are:
Prujezd zakazany: closed to all vehicles
Jednosmerny premavka: one-way traffic
Dialkova premavka: by-pass
Obchadzka: diversion
H nemocnica: hospital
Chodte vlavo: pedestrians must walk on the left.

Seat belts
If fitted, compulsory use in front and rear seats.

Signalling
Horns may be used only to warn other road users in case of danger or to signify intention to overtake. Warning may also be given by flashing the headlights. In Bratislava, the use of the horn is prohibited.

Speed limits
Built-up areas: 30mph (50kmh); *outside built-up areas*: 56mph (90kmh); *motorways*: 68mph (110kmh). Car and caravan/trailer 50mph (80kmh). The maximum speed limit for motorcyclists outside built up areas on all roads is 56mph (90kmh). Minimum speed on motorways is 31mph (50kmh).

Tolls
See page 77.

Traffic offences
Cash on-the-spot fines of up to 2000 SK are imposed.

Warning triangle
Compulsory.

GENERAL INFORMATION

Banks
Open Mon-Fri 0830-1630. Closed Sat.

Currency
Slovak crown (SK) divided into 100 hellers.

Museums
Open Tue-Sat 1000-1700. Closed Mon.

Castles
Castles are usually open fron 1 May to 31 August. Open Tue-Sat, 0900-1600/1800. Closed Mon.

Public holidays
New Year's Day; Easter Monday; May Day; National Liberation Day, 8 May; St Cyril and St Method, 5 July; Johannes Hus Festival Day, 6 July; Independence Day, 28 October; Christmas 24,25,26 Dec.

Shops
Food shops open Mon-Fri 0800-1800, Sat 0800-1200. Department stores open Mon-Fri 0800/0900-1900 (Thu 2000), Sat 0800-1500.

To make a BT Chargecard call to the UK
Dial the BT Direct number 00 42 00 44 01 to contact a BT operator in the UK who will connect the call.

Visa
British Nationals no longer require a visa.

SLOVENIA $\quad$ (SLO)

MOTORING INFORMATION

National motoring organisation
Avto-Moto Zveza Slovenije, Dunajska 128, 61113 Ljubljana. ☎ 61-181 1111.

Carriage of children
Not permitted to travel in the front seat under the age of 12.

Drinking and driving
The blood alcohol legal limit is 50mg.

Accidents and emergencies
Police ☎ 92, Fire Brigade ☎ 93, Ambulance ☎ 94.
In the event of an accident, the police must be called. A visitor must obtain a certificate from the police, detailing damage to the vehicle, in order to facilitate export from the country.

Drivers
The minimum age for drivers is 18.

Driving licence
UK driving licence accepted.

First aid kit
Compulsory.

Fuel
Service stations at entry points and on motorways are open 24 hours, otherwise 0700-2000 Monday to Saturday. *Leaded petrol*: Super (98 octane) available. *Unleaded petrol*: 91 and 95 octane available from most service stations. *Credit cards*: not accepted. *Spare fuel*: importation of spare fuel is prohibited.

Lighting
Spare bulbs must be carried. Motorcyclists must use headlights day and night.

Seat belts
If fitted, compulsory use in front and rear seats.

Speed limits
Motorcycle, car, car and caravan: in *built-up areas* the limit is 37mph (60kmh); *outside built-up areas* 50mph (80kmh). Motorways, motorcycles and cars, 75mph (120kmh); cars and caravans, 50mph (80kmh).
Tolls
See page 77.
Traffic offences
Police are empowered to impose on-the-spot fines which must be paid in the national currency.
Vehicle insurance
Croatia Insurance Company has appointed Dalmatian and Istrian Travel Ltd* to provide insurance and compulsory Green Card cover to all motorists travelling to Slovenia and Croatia.
*Dalmatian and Istrian Travel Ltd, 28 Denmark Street, London WC2H 8NJ, ☎ 0171-379 6249.
Warning triangle
Compulsory.

GENERAL INFORMATION
Banks
Open Mon-Fri 0800-1800, Sat 0800-1200.
Currency
The currency is the Tolar. Foreign currency may be exchanged at all international border crossings, and in all major towns at tourist agencies, hotels and banks.
Photography
It is prohibited to take photographs in sensitive areas, eg railways, airports, bridges, etc.
Public holidays
1, 2 Jan; Culture Day, 8 Feb; Easter Monday; Resistance Day, 27 April; Labour Days, 1, 2 May; Statehood Day, 25 June; Assumption Day, 15 Aug; Reformation Day, 31 Oct; Rememberance Day, 1 Nov; Christmas, 25 Dec; Independence Day, 26 Dec.
Shops
Open Mon-Fri 0730-1900, Sat 0730-1300.
To make a BT Chargecard call to the UK
Contact the local operator and ask for a Chargecard call to the UK.

SPAIN   E

MOTORING INFORMATION
National motoring organisation
Real Automóvil Club de España (RACE), José Abascal 10, 28003 Madrid. ☎ 447 3200. Office hours: Mon-Thurs 0830-1730, Fri 0830-1430.
Accidents and emergencies
In the case of an emergency in Madrid, Barcelona or other main town, Police ☎ 091, medical assistance ☎ 092, Fire Brigade ☎ 080. Elsewhere consult the telephone directory.
The Traffic Control Department operates an assistance service for road accidents, which includes a telephone network on motorways and some other roads. Drivers in need of assistance should ask the operator for *auxilio en carretera*.
Carriage of children
Children under 12 travelling in the front of a vehicle must be seated in an approved child seat, otherwise they must be seated in the rear of a vehicle.
Crash helmets
Compulsory for motorcyclists and passengers on machines over 125cc.
Drinking and driving
The blood alcohol legal limit is 80mg.
Drivers
The minimum age for drivers is 18.
Driving licence
EC format pink/green licence accepted; old-style green licence accepted only if accompanied by an International Driving Permit.
Fuel
Leaded petrol: Regular (92 octane) and Super (97 octane) available. *Unleaded petrol*: Regular (95 octane) available; pump legend *gasolina sin plomo*. Most readily found at the popular tourist resorts between Costa del Sol and Costa Brava, at Autopista service areas, and in the Burgos-Bilbao area. *Credit cards*: accepted at some petrol stations. *Spare fuel*: 10 litres of petrol in a can may be imported duty free.
Glasses
Motorists who wear glasses for driving should ensure that a spare pair is carried in the vehicle.
Internal ferries
Compania Transmediterranea SA operate all-year car ferry services to the Balearic and Canary Islands on the following routes:
Balearic Islands: Barcelona/Valencia to Palma (Mallorca), Mahón (Menorca) and Ibiza. There is an inter-island service from Palma to Mahón and Ibiza.
Canary Islands: Cádiz to Las Palmas (Gran Canaria) and Santa Cruz (Tenerife). Inter-island services to Fuerteventura, Lanzarote, Gomera, Hierro and La Palma. The UK agent for reservations and tickets is Southern Ferries, 179 Piccadilly, London W1V 9DB, ☎ 0171-491 4968.

Lighting
The use of dipped headlights is compulsory at night on motorways and fast roads, even if well lit. It is compulsory for motorcycles to use lights at all times. Motor vehicles must have their lights on in tunnels. A spare set of light bulbs must be carried.

Mirrors
Temporarily imported vehicles should have a minimum of two rear-view mirrors. Drivers must have a clear rear view of at least 50 metres, and caravans should therefore be equipped with extension mirrors.

Overtaking
Outside built-up areas, signal your intention to overtake by sounding your horn in the daytime, or by flashing headlights at night. The overtaking motorist must use his indicators when doing so.

The driver of a commercial vehicle will switch on his nearside flashing indicator when he thinks it is safe for you to overtake (this is the one next to the right-hand verge). While this light is flashing, it is safe to pass, but if there is danger ahead he will switch off, and he will flash his offside light until the road is clear to pass.

Stationary trams may not be overtaken when passengers are boarding or alighting.

Parking
Follow the usual restrictions on parking. On uneven dates in one-way streets in towns, vehicles should be parked on the side of the road where the houses bear uneven numbers. On the side where houses bear even numbers, parking is allowed on even dates. Do park facing the same direction as the traffic flow on that side. Parking meters and traffic wardens operate in Madrid and Barcelona.

Blue Zones, *zona azul*, are indicated by signs. Maximum period of parking between 0800 and 2100 is $1\frac{1}{2}$ hours. Discs are available from hotels, town halls and travel agencies. In the centre of some large towns there is a *zona ORA* where parking is allowed only against tickets bought in tobacconists; tickets are valid for 30, 60 or 90 minutes. Vehicles parked against regulations may be removed.

Pedestrian crossings
Jay walking is not permitted. In main towns pedestrians may not cross a road unless a traffic light is at red against the traffic, or a policeman gives permission. Offenders can be fined on the spot.

Priority
Traffic coming from the right has priority. When entering a major road from a minor one, where there is normally a sign *Stop* or *Ceda el Paso* (give way), traffic from both directions on the major road has priority. Trams and emergency vehicles always have priority.

Road signs
Most are as the international pattern. Other signs are:
Ceda el Paso: give way
Cuidado: take care
Obras: roadworks
Peligro: danger

Seat belts
If fitted, compulsory use in front and rear seats.

Signalling
Do warn road users of your whereabouts by horn or light signals. Do not make unnecessary use of horns. In urban areas horns may only be used in an emergency.

Speed limits
Built-up areas: 31mph (50kmh); *outside built-up areas*: 56-62mph (90-100kmh); *motorways*: 74mph (120kmh). In residential areas the maximum speed is 12mph (20kmh). For the purpose of overtaking outside built-up areas, it is permitted to increase speed limits by 12mph (20kmh). Cars towing a caravan or trailer, 50mph (80kmh) on dual carriageways and motorways, 44mph (70kmh) on other roads.

Tolls
Payable on certain roads (see page 76).

Traffic lights
As in the UK, but two red lights mean 'No Entry'.

Traffic offences
Police can impose on-the-spot fines of up to 50,000 Ptas. A fine can be contested within 15 days. Visiting motorists must pay immediately unless they can give the name of a person or company in Spain who will guarantee payment, otherwise the vehicle will be impounded until the fine is paid. However, except in certain cases, there is a standard reduction in the fine of 20% for immediate settlement. A *Boletin de Denuncia* is issued specifying the offence and the amount of the fine. You should check carefully that the amount written tallies with the amount paid. There are instructions in English on the back of the form for an appeal. This must be made within ten days and you should not delay until your return home. You may write in English. If the police take no action about your protest, that is the end of the matter.

Warning triangle
For vehicles with nine or more seats, or over 3,500kg weight, it is compulsory to carry two warning triangles.

GENERAL INFORMATION

Banks
Open Mon-Fri 0900-1400, Sat 0900-1300 in some towns.

Currency
Peseta.

Museums
Tue-Sat 0900/1000-1300/1400 and 1500/1600-1800/2000. Sun 0900/1000-1400. Entry to state museums is free on Saturdays, after 1430 on Sundays and on the following days: 18 May, 6 and 12 Dec.

Public holidays
New Year's Day; Epiphany; St Joseph's Day, 19 Mar*; Maundy Thursday*; Good Friday; Easter Monday; Labour Day; St James Day, 25 July*; Assumption 15 Aug; National Day, 12 Oct; All Saints Day, 1 Nov; Constitution

Day, 6 Dec; Immaculate Conception, 8 Dec; Christmas Day. *not observed in all provinces.

Shops
Open Mon-Sat 0900/1000-1300/1330 and 1500/1530-1930/2000.

To make a BT Chargecard call to the UK
Dial the BT Direct number 900 99 0044 to contact a BT operator in the UK who will connect the call. Available from most phones.

SWEDEN

S

MOTORING INFORMATION

National motoring organisations
Motormännens Riksförbund (M), *AIT*, Sveavägen 159, 10435 Stockholm. ☎ 8-690 38 00. Office hours: Mon-Fri 0830-1700.
Kungl Automobil Klubben (KAK), *FIA*, Gyllenstiernsgatan 4, S-11526, Stockholm. ☎ 0860 0055. Office hours: Mon-Thurs 0900-1600, Fri 0900-1300.

Accidents and emergencies
Police, Fire Brigade and Ambulance ☎ 112. Do not leave the scene of an accident if you are involved.

Breakdowns
In the case of breakdown, motorists may contact the alarm service (Larmtjänst), ☎ (020) 910 040.

Carriage of children
Children aged seven or under should be seated in a special child restraint, or in a seat which allows them to use normal seat belts.

Climbing lanes
A climbing lane in Sweden is an extra lane sometimes provided on steep hills to the right of the regular lane. The lane allows easy overtaking of slow-moving vehicles, and it merges with the regular lane a short way past the end of the climb. It should not be confused with slow lanes in other countries.

Crash helmets
Compulsory for motorcyclists and passengers.

Drinking and driving
The blood alcohol legal limit is 20mg.

Drivers
The minimum age for drivers is 18.

Driving licence
UK driving licence accepted.

Fuel
The normal opening hours of petrol stations are 0700-1900. In most cities, near motorways and along main roads, petrol stations will remain open until 2000/2200 or even 24 hours. Outside open hours, petrol stations

are equipped with automatic pumps ('*sedel automat*') which accept bank notes. Self-serve pumps – '*Tanka Själv*'. *Leaded petrol*: low-lead 96 octane called '*Normal*' and super 98 octane called '*Premium*'. *Unleaded petrol*: 95 octane, pump legend '*Blyfrei 95*', 98 octane, pump legend '*Blyfre 98* (not sold at all petrol stations). Both fuels dispensed from green pumps. *Diesel*: rarely available at self-service pumps. Ideally, diesel should be purchased during normal working hours. *Credit cards*: generally accepted, but at 24-hour service stations on main roads and in major towns, payment must be made with 20 or 100 Crown notes. *Spare fuel*: motorists are allowed to carry up to 30 litres in cans. Petrol imported in spare cans is subject to payment of duty/VAT.

Lighting
All motor vehicles must use dipped headlights day and night all year round.

Motorways
There are no petrol stations or service areas on motorways however facilities are signposted at motorway exits.

Overtaking
Many roads in Sweden have wide shoulders – if you are driving slower than other traffic, or if you are driving a very wide vehicle, you are allowed to move out onto the shoulder to make it easier for other people to overtake you, but do not use the shoulder as another traffic lane. If you drive onto the shoulder, give way to vehicles behind you before driving back onto the road again, as you will be held responsible for any accident. Do not force another vehicle onto the shoulder if you wish to overtake it – no vehicle is obliged to move onto the shoulder.
On some narrow roads there are warning lines – elongated markings at short intervals, instead of unbroken lines. These mean that visibility is limited in one or both directions. You may cross a warning line, so long as you can cross safely and do not break the

rules for overtaking. For instance, you may cross a warning line to pass a pedestrian, a cyclist, or a stationary or slow-moving vehicle.

Trams should be overtaken on the right if the position of the tracks so permit. If there is no refuge at a tram stop, motorists should stop and give way to passengers boarding and alighting from the tram. There are trams in Göteborg, Malmo and Norrköping.

Parking

Vehicles parked on the carriageway must be on the right-hand side of the road. If in doubt about local regulations ask the police. Do not park or stop on motorways or arterial roads other than in the parking areas provided. Do observe local parking restrictions. Maps showing parking regulations in Stockholm and some other towns may be obtained from the motoring organisations or through the local authority concerned. Parking meters are in use in several larger towns, usually from 0800 to 1800. The permitted parking time varies, but is generally two hours and is always indicated on the meter. Parking fees vary according to locality, usually 5-10 SEK per hour. Fines are imposed for illegal parking.

Pedestrian crossings

Do give pedestrians the right of way on a pedestrian crossing. Pedestrians must use official crossings. It is an offence for them to cross the road against a red light.

Priority

Give way to vehicles already on a priority road before you enter it, also when you leave a petrol station, car park, camping site, or similar area. At other road junctions give way to traffic coming from the right, unless there is a road sign to the contrary. When turning left give way to oncoming traffic. When you see a 'Stop' sign, you must stop at a point where you can see up and down the other road (usually at the stop line), and you must give way to any traffic approaching along it. At most roundabouts, traffic already on the roundabout has priority and this is clearly indicated by signposting. Do give trams priority.

Seat belts

If fitted, compulsory use in front and rear seats.

Signalling

Do give warning of your approach by using the horn, or by light signals, where this is necessary to prevent an accident. In built-up areas, do not give audible warning, unless it is essential to prevent an accident.

Speed limits

Built-up areas: 31mph (50kmh); *outside built-up areas*: 44-56mph (70-90kmh); *motorways*: 68mph (110kmh), reduced to 56mph (90kmh) on certain stretches around major towns – these limits are always signposted. Car and trailer/caravan with effective braking system, 50mph (80kmh).

Traffic offences

Swedish police are authorised to impose, but not collect, fines on the spot in cases of violation of traffic regulations. Fines range from 300 to 1,200 SEK, but if two or more offences are committed and total fines exceed 2,500 SEK, the offender will be taken to court. Some fineable offences are: registration plate dirty or missing; exceeding the speed limit; driving without lights in daylight; not having a warning triangle or GB plate.

Warning triangle

Advisable.

GENERAL INFORMATION

Banks

Open 0930-1500. City centres – bank open until 1800.

Currency

Swedish Crown (SEK).

Museums

Opening hours vary but are generally 0930/1000 - 1500/1600. Most museums are closed on Mondays.

Public holidays

New Year's Day; Epiphany; Good Friday; Easter Monday; Labour Day; Ascension; Whit Sunday; Whit Monday; Midsummer (Sat between 20 and 26 June); All Saints, (Sat between 31 Oct and 6 Nov); Christmas, 24, 25, 26 Dec.

Shops

Open Mon-Fri 0900-1800, Sat 0900-1300/1600, although hours vary throughout the week. In some large towns, department stores remain open until 1900/2000.

To make a BT Chargecard call to the UK

Dial the BT Direct number 155 2444 to contact a BT operator in the UK who will connect the call. Available from most phones.

SWITZERLAND

MOTORING INFORMATION

National motoring organisations

Automobile Club de Suisse (ACS), *FIA*,
39 Wasserwerkgasse, 3000 Bern 13. ☎ (031) 328 31 11.
Office hours: Mon-Fri 0800-1200 and 1400-1730.
Touring Club Suisse (TCS), *AIT*, 9 rue Pierre Fatio,
1211 Genève 3. ☎ (022) 737 12 12. Road & Touring
Information, ☎ (022) 735 80 00. Office hours: Mon-Fri
0800/0900-1145/1200 and 1300/1400-1700/1900,
according to office and season. Sat 0800/0915-
1100/1200 and 1330-1700, according to office and
season. Head Office closed Sat.

Accidents and emergencies

Police ☎ 117, Fire Brigade ☎ 118, Ambulance
☎ 117 or 144 in Genève, Zürich, Bern, Basel, Interlaken,
Winterthur and other major towns.

Carriage of children

Children under seven years of age may not travel in the
front seat, unless an approved child restraint is fitted.

Crash helmets

Compulsory for motorcyclists and passengers.

Drinking and driving

The blood alcohol legal limit is 80mg.

Drivers

The minimum age for drivers is 18.

Driving licence

UK driving licence accepted.

Fuel

On motorways, service stations are usually open 0600-
2200/2400, with the exception of Basel North, Pratteln
North/South, and Coldrerio East/West (N2) which are
open 24 hours. On normal roads, usual opening hours
are 0600/0700-2000; smaller stations are open
0700/0800-1800. A few service stations open 24 hours
during the summer. Outside these hours, petrol is
widely available from 24-hour automatic pumps, which
accept 10 or 20 SF notes.
Leaded petrol: Super (98 octane) available. *Unleaded
petrol*: Super (95 octane) available; pump legend
bleifrei, essence sans plomb or *benzina sensa piomba*.
Credit cards: accepted. *Spare fuel*: 25 litres of petrol in
a can may be imported duty free.

Internal ferries

A car ferry operates across Lake Lucerne between
Beckenreid and Gersau (April-October), and across
Lake Zürich between Horgen and Meilen (all year).
There are also international ferry services to Germany
across Lake Constance (Bodensee) from Romanshorn
to Frederichshafen and from Constance to Meersburg.

Lighting

Do use sidelights after nightfall or in thick fog if the
vehicle is stationary, except if parked where there is
sufficient street lighting, or in an authorised car park.
Dipped headlights are compulsory in tunnels.
Motorcyclists should use lights at all times.

Motorways

Signposted in green. All vehicles using the motorway
network must display a vignette (see page 33). Motel
accommodation is available at a number of locations on
the network.

Mountain roads

Take extra care when travelling on mountain roads. You
must be able to pull up within half the distance of clear
vision, especially when negotiating a blind bend. When
two vehicles meet on a narrow mountain road, the
descending car must keep to the extreme right-hand
side of the road and even stop or go into reverse if
necessary.
Mountain postal roads are indicated by a sign with the
traditional post-horn in yellow on a blue rectangle. On
these roads, postal vehicles have priority. The same sign
with the addition of a red diagonal stripe indicates the
end of the postal road. Drivers of private cars must pull
up if signalled to do so by postal coach drivers.
A sign showing a disc with a wheel and chains in the
centre indicates that snow chains are necessary for the
mountain road ahead.
Some mountain postal roads are one-way only. This is
indicated by a white rectangle beneath the blue
rectangle with the yellow horn. On others during
certain hours, one-way single file traffic is in operation.
Circulation hours in both directions are posted at each
end of the road.

Overtaking

Overtake on the left. When overtaking, it is compulsory
to signal right before returning to the right-hand lane. A
moving tram must be overtaken on the right if there is
sufficient room; if not, the vehicle may be overtaken on
the left. Overtake a stationary tram or train on the right
only if there is a refuge. If not, overtake on the left only
if there is no danger to traffic. Motorcyclists must not
overtake a column of vehicles or weave between
vehicles.

Parking

Do not park where there is a sign *Stationierungsverbot*
or *Interdiction de Stationner* (no parking) or where
parking might hinder traffic. Motorists with parking
discs may park in Blue Zones free. Parking discs can be
obtained free from ACS and TCS offices, and in some
towns with Blue Zones (Basel, Bern, Genève), discs can
be obtained from most petrol stations, garages, kiosks,
restaurants and police stations.

Ensure that your vehicle is really immobilised by leaving it in bottom or reverse gear, according to the way the vehicle is facing, by use of a chock, or by turning the front wheels towards the kerb. Wheel clamps may be used on illegally parked vehicles. Parking on pavements is forbidden unless authorised by specific signs. The resorts of Murren, Wengen, Zermatt, Braunwald and Rigi are inaccessible by car. Parking facilities are located at railway stations, and journeys may be completed by public transport.

Priority

All main roads are marked in the centre by a white line. When the road is clear, a broken white line may be crossed when overtaking or turning left. Do not cross a double white line. In open country, main road traffic has right of way over that entering from secondary roads. In built-up areas, traffic entering from the right has priority. Trams have right of way on all roads.

The international priority sign is placed on most secondary highways where they intersect with main roads having priority. Blue posts indicate a main road. In built-up areas, buses have priority when leaving a bus-stop.

Seat belts

If fitted, compulsory use in front and rear seats.

Signalling

Do not use a horn unnecessarily, and only with consideration in residential areas. After dark, use your headlamp flasher instead of the horn unless there is an emergency.

Speed limits

Built-up areas: 31mph (50kmh); *outside built-up areas*: 50mph (80kmh); *motorways*: 62-74mph (100-120kmh). Cars towing a caravan or trailer: up to 1000kg, 50mph (80kmh), outside built-up areas; over 1000kg, 37mph (60kmh), outside built-up areas, and 50mph (80kmh) on motorways.

Temporary importation of caravans

Caravans and trailers not exceeding 2.30 metres in width and 8 metres in length may be imported without formality. Caravans up to 2.50 metres wide may enter Switzerland if they are towed by a four-wheel drive vehicle or by a vehicle exceeding 3.5 tonnes: the total length of the combination must not exceed 18 metres. No authorisation is required. A number of roads are closed to touring caravans and light trailers – RAC Travel Information can provide details.

Touring information

General touring information, ☎ 111; weather reports, ☎ 162; mountain pass conditions, ☎ 163.

Traffic offences

Police are empowered to impose and collect on-the-spot fines for traffic offences.

Warning triangle

Compulsory.

GENERAL INFORMATION

Banks

Generally open Mon-Fri 0800/0830-1630/1800. In Lausanne, banks close 1230-330.

Currency

Swiss franc.

Public holidays

New Year's Day; Good Friday; Easter Monday; Ascension; Whit Monday; Christmas Day. In addition, other days are observed in some Cantons.

Shops

Open Mon-Fri 0800/0900-1830 (1845 in Genève), Sat 0800-1600/1700. Hours vary between towns.

To make a BT Chargecard call to the UK

Dial the BT Direct number 155 2444 to contact a BT operator in the UK who will connect the call. Available from all phones.

TURKEY   (TR)

MOTORING INFORMATION

National motoring organisation

Türkiye Turing Ve Otomobil Kurumu (TTOK), *FIA & AIT*, I. Oto Sanayi Sitesi Yani, Camlik Caddesi, 4. Levent, Istanbul. ☎ 212-282 81 40. Office hours: Mon-Fri 0830-1200 and 1230-1700.

Accidents and emergencies

Police ☎ 155, Fire Brigade ☎ 110, Ambulance ☎ 112. All accidents (whether there are injuries caused or not) must be reported to the police as a report has to be prepared by them for the Turkish Insurance Bureau.

Carriage of children

It is advisable for children to travel in the back seat of the vehicle.

Crash helmets

Compulsory for motorcyclists.

Drinking and driving

The blood alcohol legal limit is 50mg.

Drivers

Normally, only those 18 and over may drive but visitors holding a valid full driving licence in their country of residence, may do so even if they are under 18. They may, however, only drive foreign-registered vehicles.

Driving licence
UK driving licences are accepted for visitors driving a vehicle temporarily imported into Turkey, for visits up to three months.

Fire extinguisher
Compulsory.

First aid kit
Compulsory.

Fuel
Motorists are advised to 'top-up' their tanks at every opportunity. *Leaded petrol*: Regular (91 octane) and Super (96 octane) available. *Unleaded petrol*: Super (95 octane) available; pump legend *kursunsuz benzin*. *Credit cards*: not widely accepted. *Spare fuel*: 25 litres maximum in cans may be imported duty free.

Lighting
Dipped headlights must be used after sunset in built-up areas. A vehicle parked at the roadside after dark must display sidelights, whether or not the road is lit. However, this does not apply in built-up areas if the vehicle is visible from a distance of 150 metres.

Overtaking
Do not overtake at intersections, level crossings, curves, on bridges, in tunnels or where road signs indicate that it is forbidden.

Parking
The sign *Park Yapilmaz* indicates that parking is forbidden. Parking is not permitted on pedestrian crossings, outside garage/car park entrances, on tramways, near intersections or bends, on level crossings, underpasses, overpasses or within 25 metres of danger signs.

Priority
Except where otherwise indicated, priority must be given to vehicles coming from the right. Vehicles on a main road have priority over those entering from a secondary road.

Road signs
Most signs conform to the international pattern, but other road signs which may be seen are:
Dikkat: attention
Dur: stop
Gümrük: Customs
Hastahane: hospital
Park Yapilmaz: no parking
Tamirat: roadworks
Yavas: slow
The word *'Nufus'* (inhabitants) often appears on signs at the entrance into towns to indicate the population. *'Rakim'* indicates the altitude.

Seat belts
If fitted, compulsory in front seats and and rear seats.

Signalling
Use of the horn is forbidden unless absolute necessary.

Speed limits
Built-up areas: 31mph (50kmh); *outside built-up areas and motorways*: 56mph (90kmh). Cars towing a caravan or trailer are limited to 25mph (40kmh) in built-up areas, and 44mph (70kmh) on all other roads.

Temporary importation of vehicles
Vehicle details will be entered in the visitor's passport. The vehicle must be exported by that person. If a vehicle is imported by a person other than the owner, a letter of authorisation from the owner must be held by the driver and certified either by a lawyer or the RAC.

Tolls
See page 78.

Traffic offences
Police are empowered to impose on-the-spot fines for violations of traffic regulations.

Warning triangle
It is compulsory to carry two warning triangles.

GENERAL INFORMATION

Banks
Open Mon-Fri 0830-1200 and 1330-1700.

Currency
Turkish lira.

Museums
Open Tue-Sun 0830-1200 and 1330-1700 (winter), 0830-1730 (summer).

Photography
Photography is forbidden in certain areas as indicated by signs *Yasak Bolge* or *Yabancilara Yasaktir*.

Public holidays
New Year's Day; Seker Bayrami religious festival (moveable in March); Independence and Children's Day, 23 Apr; Youth, Sports and Atatürk Commemoration Day, 19 May; Kurban Bayrami religious festival (moveable in June); Victory Day, 30 Aug; Republic Day, 29 Oct.

Shops
Open Mon-Sat 0930-1300 and 1400-1900. Tourist shops operate similar hours.

To make a BT Chargecard call to the UK
Dial the BT Direct number 00 800 44 1177 to contact a BT operator in the UK who will connect the call. Available from all payphones.

Visa
British nationals visiting Turkey for less than three months must purchase a visa (costing £10), on arrival at the airport or frontier. Visitors are advised to provide **new** £ sterling banknotes in payment.

FROM COUNTRY TO COUNTRY
TOLL ROADS

Toll charges are correct at the time of going to press, and details for certain countries are selective. A current leaflet for countries marked (*) is available from RAC Travel Information, ☎ 0345 333 222

AUSTRIA*

As of 1 January 1997, a motorway tax disc must be displayed on all vehicles using motorways. Visitors may purchase a **weekly** (valid for a maximum of 10 days) or **monthly** (valid for 2 consecutive calendar months) disc at all major Austrian border crossings, petrol stations and post offices. Annual discs are also available. The cost, in Austrian Schillings, is as follows:

	2 month	weekly
motorcycle	80	not available
private car (with or without trailer), certain mini-buses	150	70
vehicle between 3.5–7.5 tons	1500	300

† The disc is not valid on the following motorways, although a disc entitles motorists to a 15% discount on the toll: S16 Arlberg Tunnel, A13 Brenner Motorway, A9 Pyhrn Motorway, A10 Tauern Motorway.

The major Austrian toll road companies issue multiple journey cards which allow an appreciable reduction in the price charged for a single journey. An additional charge may be made per person for over two or three people in cars or minibuses but children travel at reduced prices, sometimes free. Tolls are given in Austrian schillings. (Credit cards not accepted.)

AUSTRIA – ITALY
Timmelsjoch High Alpine Road (Passo del Rombo)

motorcycle	single	50
	return	70
car	single	80
	return	120

(trailers or caravans prohibited)

TYROL – ITALY
Brenner motorway (A13)†

motorcycle	100
car, motor caravan, minibus (up to 9 seats)	130
car with caravan or trailer	170

KITZBÜHEL – EAST TYROL
Felber Tauern Road

motorcycle	100
car, summer/winter	190/110
caravan or trailer	40

SALZBURG – TYROL
Gerlos Road

motorcycle	50
car with or without trailer	90

Grossglockner Pass

motorcycle	230
car	350
car and caravan/trailer, motor caravan	440

BLUDENZ – LANDECK
Silvretta High Alpine Road

motorcycle	80
private car per person	45
return journey on same day	70
private car, per child 6-16	20
child under 6	free
motor caravan	125

(caravans/trailers prohibited)

SALZBURG – CARINTHIA
Tauern motorway (A10)†

motorcycle		100
car, minibus (up to 9 seats)	May – October	190
	November – April	120
caravan or trailer		40

(for partial tolls through Katschberg and Radstadter Tunnels see Tunnel section)

BULGARIA

Tolls are levied on foreign registered vehicles using motorways and dual carriageways as follows:

private car	2 leva per km
minibus with up to 11 seats including the driver	3 leva per km
coach with more than 11 seats	4 leva per km

BULGARIA/ROMANIA

A toll and environmental tax is levied to use the bridge across the river Danube between Rousse in Bulgaria and Gjourguevo (*Giurgia*) in Romania. The following rates apply to foreign registered vehicles:

motorcycle	60 leva
private car	210 leva
minibus with up to 11 seats including the driver	390 leva

Environmental tax

private car	US$ 1 or DM 2
minibus	US$ 2 or DM 3.50

CROATIA

Tolls are payable on the following motorway sections. Current tariffs are available from the RAC.

E59	Zagreb – Kralovac
E59	Zagreb – Gubssevo
E70	Zagreb – Kutina
E70	Zagreb – Novska

CZECH REPUBLIC

Tolls are payable for use of motorways. A sticker, valid for 1 year, must be displayed on the front windscreen. The toll for a car up to 3,500 kg is 400 Kc.

FRANCE*

Tolls are payable on most routes, usually by taking a ticket at the point of entry and paying at the exit, although some toll barriers are operated automatically by depositing the exact toll in coins. On numerous sections of autoroute, particularly around cities and large towns, no tolls are levied. Visa and Access (Mastercard) are accepted for payment. Tolls are given in French francs.

Tolls are applied as follows:
(1) Light motor vehicle with two axles with a height less than 1.30 metres measured at right angles to the front axle, with or without a luggage trailer; family minibus with up to nine seats. (Motorcyclists pay a lower rate than this category.)
(2) Vehicle, or vehicle combination (car and trailer/caravan), with more than two axles and with a height of not more than 1.30 metres measured at right angles to the front axle.
(3) Commercial vehicle with two axles with a height of more than 1.30 metres measured at right angles to the front axle; coach with two axles; motor home; minibus, unless it has a maximum of nine seats and is for private use only, when it is charged as category (1).

Charges correct as of 2 February 1996

	(1)	(2)	(3)
A1 PARIS – LILLE (214 km)			
Autoroute du Nord			
Paris – Roye (Amiens)	33.00	49.00	56.00
Paris – Lille	56.00	84.00	91.00
A2 COMBLES (Jct A1) – BELGIAN FRONTIER (78 km)			
Bapaume – Hordain	24.00	37.00	43.00
A4 PARIS – STRASBOURG (470 km)			
Autoroute de l'Est			
Paris – Metz	114.00	174.00	200.00
Paris – Strasbourg	182.00	273.00	309.00
Calais – Strasbourg* (617km)	218.00	326.00	358.00
A5 PARIS (MELUN) – LANGRES (247 km)			
Melun (N104 – La Franciliene) – Troyes	40.00	55.00	94.00
Troyes – Semoutiers	27.00	31.00	52.00
A6 PARIS – LYON (456 km)			
Autoroute du Soleil			
Paris – Beaune	90.00	104.00	172.00
Paris – Lyon (Villefranche)	142.00	164.00	271.00
Calais – Lyon* (765 km)	265.00	349.00	488.00
A7 LYON – MARSEILLE (313 km)			
Autoroute du Soleil			
Lyon – Aix – Marseille	107.00	166.00	172.00
Calais – Marseille* (1070 km)	372.00	515.00	660.00
A8 AIX-EN-PROVENCE (Coudoux, A7) – NICE – MENTON (200 km)			
Autoroute la Provençale			
Aix-en-Provence – Menton	94.50	142.50	153.00
Calais – Nice* (1226 km)	450.00	632.50	786.00
A9 ORANGE (A7) – LE PERTHUS (280 km)			
Autoroute la Languedocienne-Catalane			
Orange – Narbonne sud	71.00	110.00	114.00
Orange – Le Perthus	106.00	165.00	172.00
Calais – Le Perthus* (1235 km)	451.00	638.00	791.00
A10 PARIS – BORDEAUX (585 km)			
Autoroute l'Aquitaine			
Paris – Tours centre	99.00	149.00	157.00
Paris – Bordeaux (Virsac)	234.00	357.00	376.00
Calais – Bordeaux (870 km)	334.00	506.00	536.00
A11 PARIS – NANTES (383 km)			
Autoroute l'Océane			
Paris – Le Mans nord	79.00	118.00	132.00
Paris – Nantes	156.00	234.00	251.00

	(1)	(2)	(3)
A13 PARIS – CAEN (225 km)			
Autoroute de Normandie			
Paris – Tancarville (Le Havre)	35.00	51.50	54.50
Paris – Caen	60.00	90.00	93.50
A16 BELGIAN BORDER – CALAIS – BOULOGNE – PARIS			
Paris (L'Isle-Adam N1) – Amiens			
	41.00	54.00	82.00
A26 CALAIS – TROYES (400 km)			
Autoroute des Anglais			
Calais – Reims	93.00	139.00	153.00
Reims – Troyes	42.00	60.00	84.00
A31 BEAUNE – LUXEMBOURG (364 km)			
Beaune – Dijon	7.00	8.00	12.00
Dijon – Toul (Gye)	61.00	70.00	125.00
A36 BEAUNE – MULHOUSE (232 km)			
La Comtoise			
Beaune – Besançon centre	25.00	29.00	48.00
Paris – Mulhouse (535 km)	168.00	195.00	321.00
A39 DIJON – DOLE (42 km)			
Crimolois (A31) – Choisey (A36)	13.00	15.00	24.00
A40 MACON – LE FAYET (212 km)			
Calais – Genève* (842 km)	312.00	435.00	594.00
Calais – Le Fayet* (895 km)	339.00	462.00	621.00
A41 GRENOBLE – SCIENTRIER (130 km)			
Grenoble – Chambéry	25.00	40.00	40.00
Chambéry – Scentrier (A41)	42.00	65.00	65.00
A42 LYON – PONT D'AIN (A40) (64 km)			
	18.00	21.00	34.00
A43/A431 LYON – ALBERTVILLE (150 km)			
Lyon – Les Abrets	30.00	47.00	47.00
Lyon – Albertville	96.00	149.00	149.00
A48 BOURGOIN (A43) – GRENOBLE (49 km)			
Bourgoin – Grenoble	27.00	41.00	41.00
Calais – Grenoble* (869 km)	312.00	422.00	561.00
A49 GRENOBLE – VALENCE			
Tullins – Bourg de Péage	33.00	50.00	50.00
A50 MARSEILLE – TOULON (62 km)			
	19.00	28.50	30.50
A51 AIX-EN-PROVENCE – SISTERON (103 km)			
Autoroute du Val de Durance			
Aix-en-Provence – Sisteron	44.00	66.50	72.50

	(1)	(2)	(3)
A52 CHATEAUNEUF-LE-ROUGE (A8) – AUBAGNE (A50) (15 km)			
Aix-en-Provence – Aubagne	16.00	24.00	25.50
A54 ARLES – NIMES OUEST (24 km)			
	10.00	16.00	16.00
A57 TOULON – LE CANNET DES MAURES (A8)			
	20.50	31.00	31.00
A61 TOULOUSE – NARBONNE SUD (150 km)			
Autoroute des Deux-Mers	59.00	91.00	98.00
A62 BORDEAUX – TOULOUSE (244 km)			
Autoroute des Deux-Mers	87.00	135.00	145.00
A63 BORDEAUX – SPANISH FRONTIER (192 km)			
Autoroute de la Côte Basque			
St Geours de Marenne – Biriatou			
	39.50	60.00	60.00
A64 BAYONNE – TARBES (149 km)			
La Pyrénéenne			
Sames – Tarbes est	52.00	80.00	85.00
A71 ORLEANS – CLERMONT FERRAND (293 km)			
Orléans centre – Bourges	47.00	72.00	74.00
Bourges – Clermont Ferrand	64.00	75.00	121.00
Calais – C. Ferrand (687 km)	262.00	368.00	432.00
A72 CLERMONT FERRAND – ST ETIENNE (140 km)	51.00	79.00	86.00
A81 LE MANS (Joué-en-Charnie) – LAVAL (La Gravelle) (84 km)	29.00	41.00	44.00
Paris – La Gravelle (278 km)	128.00	188.00	210.00
A83 NANTES – NIORT (136km)			
Nantes (La Cour Neuve) – Fontenay-le-Comte			
	38.00	59.00	65.00

* Via A26 Autoroute des Anglais

Tolls are charged for crossing the following bridges:

Tancarville Bridge

motorcycle	free
car	13.00
car and caravan	16.00

Normandie Bridge (A29)

motorcycle	free
car	32.00
car and trailer	37.00

GREECE*

Tolls are levied on several routes, and are given in Drachmas. Tolls are applied as follows:

(1) Motorcycle, scooter
(2) Passenger car; minibus with up to 10 seats
(3) Motor caravan
(4) Car and caravan

	(1)	(2)	(3)	(4)
Athína – Kórinthos	250	500	800	1000
Kórinthos – Pátrai	250	600	1000	1000
Kórinthos – Trípolis	500	900	1200	1500
Athína – Lamía	550	900	1400	1600
Lamía – Lárisa	250	500	800	1000
Lárisa – Kateríni	250	500	800	1000
Kateríni – Thessaloniki	250	500	1000	1000

HUNGARY

Tolls are levied on the section of the M1 between Györ and the Austrian border (Hegyeshalom) as follows:
motorcycle, car with/without trailer
(not exceeding 1.90m in height)   1300 forints

ITALY*

Toll tickets are collected on entry to the motorway system and paid on exit. Major credit cards are accepted in payment on the A4, A22, A28 and A32 only. Motorists may pay tolls with a Viacard on the majority of motorways (except A18 and A20). The card can be used for any vehicle and is available in two amounts: 50,000 lire and 90,000 lire. Motorists may obtain it from motorway toll booths and service areas, certain banks, tourist offices and tobacconists. When leaving a motorway on which the Viacard is accepted, the motorist gives his card and entry ticket to the attendant who will deduct the amount due. At motorway exits with automatic barriers, the Viacard should be inserted into the machine. The card is valid until the credit expires. Credit cards are not accepted for payment of the Viacard. Full details are available from RAC Travel Information, ☎ 0345 333 222. Tolls are given in Lire and correct as of September 1996 but subject to increase in 1997.

Tolls are applied as follows:
(1) Motorcycle; car with a height measured at the front axle of less than 1.30 metres.
(2) Three-wheeled vehicle; vehicle with a height at the front axle exceeding 1.30 metres.
(3) Vehicle (with/without trailer) with three axles.
(4) Vehicle (with/without trailer) with four axles.
(5) Vehicle (with/without trailer) with five axles.

	(1)	(2)	(3)	(4)	(5)

A1 MILANO – NAPOLI
Milano – Bologna

	(1)	(2)	(3)	(4)	(5)
Milano – Bologna	16500	17000	21000	33000	39500

	(1)	(2)	(3)	(4)	(5)
Milano – Roma (ring road)	45500	46500	58000	91000	109000
Milano – Napoli	62500	64000	78500	124000	148500

A3 NAPOLI – REGGIO CALABRIA
Napoli – Salerno

	(1)	(2)	(3)	(4)	(5)
Napoli – Salerno	1500	1900	3000	4000	5000

A4 TORINO – TRIESTE
Torino – Milano(Ghisolfa)

	(1)	(2)	(3)	(4)	(5)
Torino – Milano(Ghisolfa)	10000	10000	12500	20000	24000
Milano – Mestre (Venezia)	21500	22000	27000	43000	51500

A5 MONTE BIANCO (Mt. Blanc Tunnel) – TORINO
Aosta – Torino

	(1)	(2)	(3)	(4)	(5)
Aosta – Torino	17500	19500	26000	41000	47500
Aosta – Santhià (A4)	15500	16500	22500	35500	41000

A6 TORINO – SAVONA (A10)

	(1)	(2)	(3)	(4)	(5)
	13500	14000	19000	29500	34000

A7 MILANO – GENOVA

	(1)	(2)	(3)	(4)	(5)
	12000	12500	15500	24500	29000

A8/9 MILANO – SESTO CALENDE

	(1)	(2)	(3)	(4)	(5)
	3600	3600	4500	7500	8500

A8/9 MILANO – COMO

	(1)	(2)	(3)	(4)	(5)
	4200	4200	5000	8500	10000

A10 GENOVA – FRENCH BORDER
Genova – Savona Vado

	(1)	(2)	(3)	(4)	(5)
Genova – Savona Vado	4000	4000	5000	8000	10000
Savona Vado – French Border	19500	23500	37000	48500	56000

A11 FIRENZE – PISA

	(1)	(2)	(3)	(4)	(5)
	6500	6500	8000	13000	15500

A12 GENOVA – CECINA
Genova – Rosignano M.

	(1)	(2)	(3)	(4)	(5)
Genova – Rosignano M.	25000	26000	34000	54000	63000
Roma – Citavecchia	5000	5000	6000	10000	12000

A13 BOLOGNA – PADOVA (A4)

	(1)	(2)	(3)	(4)	(5)
	9500	9500	12000	18500	22500

A14 BOLOGNA – TARANTO
Bologna – Pescara (A25)

	(1)	(2)	(3)	(4)	(5)
Bologna – Pescara (A25)	26000	27000	33000	52000	63000

	(1)	(2)	(3)	(4)	(5)
Bologna – Taranto	58500	60000	73500	116500	139500

A15 PARMA – LA SPEZIA

	13000	13500	18000	28500	33000

A16 NAPOLI – CANOSA

	21500	22000	27000	42500	51000

A18 MESSINA – CATANIA

	5000	6000	9500	12500	14500

A20 MESSINA – PALERMO

Messina – Furiano

	9500	10000	11500	18500	22500

Cefalù – Buonfornello (A19)

	1300	1300	1500	2500	3000

A21 TORINO – BRESCIA

Torino – Piacenza (A1)

	14500	14500	18000	28500	34500

Piacenza – Bréscia (A4)

	6000	6000	7500	12000	14500

A22 BRENNERO – MODENA

Brénnero – Verona (A4)

	21500	22000	27000	42500	51000

Brénnero – Módena

	28500	29500	36000	57000	68500

A23 PALMANOVA – TARVISIO

Palmanova (A4) – Udine N.

	2100	2100	2600	4100	4900

Udine N. – Tarvísio

	8500	8500	10500	16500	20000

A24 ROMA – L'AQUILA – TERAMO

	12000	12500	14000	23500	28500

A25 ROMA – PESCARA

	14000	14500	16500	27500	33500

A26 GENOVA – ARONA

	14500	14500	18000	28500	34000

A27 MESTRE – BELLUNO

Mestre N. – Vittorio Veneto N.

	6000	6500	8000	12500	15000

A30 CASERTA – SALERNO

	4500	5000	6000	9500	11500

A31 VICENZA – PIOVENE ROCCHETTE

	2500	2500	3000	4500	5500

A32 FREJUS TUNNEL – TORINO

	12700	14700	22700	30500	35500

NETHERLANDS

Tolls are payable on the following, and are given in Florins.

Kiltunnel (Dordecht – Hoekse)
motorcycle, car (with/without trailer)   3.50

Waalbridge (Prins Willem Alexander Bridge)
motorcycle/car (up to 800kg)   2.90
car (over 800kg)   3.50

Zeeland Bridge   TOLL FREE

NORWAY

On the E6 west of Oslo, there is a toll charge of 10 Kroner near Drammen.

PORTUGAL*

On the 25 de Abril Bridge, which links Lisboa with the south bank of the River Tagus at the Lisboa end of the Vila Franca de Xira motorway, toll charges are levied, for most of the year, on northbound traffic only.

Tolls are levied on the following auto-estradas out of Lisboa, and are given in Escudos. Correct August 1996. Tolls are applied as follows:

(1) Motorcycles and vehicles with an axle height less than 1.10 metres (with or without trailer).

(2) Vehicles with two axles, with an axle height exceeding 1.10 metres.

(3) Vehicles with three axles, with an axle height exceeding 1.10 metres.

		(1)	(2)	(3)
A1	Lisboa – Santarém (64 km)	470	820	1060
	Santarém – Fatima (49 km)	510	890	1140
	Fatima – Coimbra (76 km)	760	1330	1700
	Coimbra – Aveiro (44 km)	380	670	860
	Aveiro – Porto (71 km)	570	1000	1280
A2	Lisboa – Marateca (48 km)	390	690	870
A3	Porto – Braga (51 km)	380	700	900
A4	Porto – Amarante (53 km)	500	890	1160
A5	Lisboa – Cascais (25 km)	160	340	340
A6	Marateca – Montemor-o-Novo (44 km)	550	950	1230
A8	Lisboa – Torres Vedras (37 km)	300	710	910

SLOVAKIA

Tolls are payable for use of certain motorways. A sticker valid for 1 year must be displayed on the front windscreen and for a private car costs 200 or 400 Sk. according to cylinder capacity. Available at border crossings.

SLOVENIA

Tolls are payable on the following motorway sections. Current tariffs are available from the RAC.

A1/E63 Ljubljana – Kranj
A10/E70 Ljubljana – Razdrto
A10/E57 Maribor – Celje

SPAIN*

The following tolls apply to motorcycles and private cars (with/without a caravan); given in Pesetas. Tolls correct September 1996 but subject to increase in 1977.

A1 Burgos (Castañares) – Miranda de Ebro (A68)1145
A2 Junction A7 – Zaragoza (Alfajarin)   2205
A4 Sevilla (Dos Hermanas) – Cadiz (Puerto Real)1345
A6 Madrid (Villalba) – Adanero   1075
A7 La Jonquera – Barcelona N.   1345
    Barcelona S. – Salou   1270
    Salou – Valencia (Puzol)   3385
    Valencia (Silla) – Alicante (San Juan)   2240
A8 Bilbao (Basauri) – San Sebastian   1655
    San Sebastian – French border   215
A9 La Coruña – Santiago de Compostela   580
    Pontevedra – Vigo   415
A15 Pamplona (Noain) – Tudela   1245
A18 Barcelona – Manresa   710†
A19 Barcelona – Malgrat de Mar   440
A66 Oveido (Campomanes) – Leon   1290
A68 Bilbao – Zaragoza   4755
† motorcycle 355

	Cat. 1	Cat. 2	Cat. 3
Garraf Tunnel (A16)	300	620	1095
(between Barcelona and Sitges)			
Vallvidrera Tunnel	340	430	685
(near Barcelona)			

Cat.1   motorcycle
Cat. 2 car, car with trailer, van, minibus
Cat. 3 car and caravan

TURKEY

Tolls are charged on the following routes:

Edirne – Istanbul	Tsarsus – Pozanti
Istanbul – Izmit	Ankara – Gerede
Gebze – Izmit	Izmir – Çesme

Tolls are levied on the Bosphorus Bridge and Fatih Sultan Mehmet Bridge, payable in the direction Europe to Asia only, as follows:

motorcycle	20,000 TRL
car, minibus	50,000 TRL

TUNNELS

In many countries it is an offence to drive through a tunnel without headlights. At the exit, police may impose an on-the-spot fine.
*In Austria, vehicles displaying a valid motorway tax disc receive a 15% discount on tunnel tolls.

ALBULA,SWITZERLAND

Rail tunnel: Thusis,Tiefencastel,Samedan. There are at least five services daily in cach direction.
Rates

car	85 Sw F
car with caravan	140 Sw F
	plus 10–50 Sw F per passenger

ARLBERG, AUSTRIA*

The 14km-long road tunnel is parallel to and south of the Arlberg Pass. It is usually open all through the year but when it is closed, vehicle/trailer combinations may be transported through the Arlberg rail tunnel between Langen and St Anton. Reservations should be made at least three hours before departure of the train, ☎ Langen 05582 201 or ☎ St Anton 05446 2242.
Rates (road tunnel)

motorcycle	AS 100
car, motor caravan, minibus (up to 9 seats)	AS 150
car with caravan or trailer	AS 210

BIELSA, FRANCE/SPAIN

The three km-long road tunnel through the Pyrénées between Aragnouet and Bielsa is usually open year round. The tunnel is closed at night and subject to sudden closure, depending on weather conditions, at other times.

BOSRUCK (A9 Pyhrn Autobahn), AUSTRIA*

This road tunnel is 5.5 km long and runs between Spital am Pyhrn and Selzthal, to the east of the Pyhrn Pass. It forms part of the Pyhrn Autobahn between Linz and Graz.
Rates

motorcycle	AS	60
car, minibus (up to 9 seats)	AS	70
caravan or trailer	AS	30

CADI, SPAIN

The 5km-long tunnel between Bellver de Cerdanya and Bagá on the C1411, to the west of the Tosas Pass.
Rates (correct September 1996)

motorcycle	1030 Ptas
car with or without baggage trailer	1280 Ptas
car and caravan	2795 Ptas

FREJUS, FRANCE/ITALY

The road tunnel between Modane and Bardonecchia is 12.8 km long and is open all year. Tolls are similar to the

Mont Blanc tunnel. Sidelights must be used.
Speed limits: min 60kph – max 80kph.

GLEINALM (A9 PYHRN AUTOBAHN), AUSTRIA*
The road tunnel between St Michael and Friesach, near Graz, is 8.3 km long and forms part of the A9 road from Linz to Slovenia.
Rates

motorcycle	AS 100
car, minibus (up to 9 seats)	AS 130
caravan or trailer	AS 30

GREAT ST BERNARD, SWITZERLAND/ITALY
The road tunnel between Bourg St Pierre and Aosta (*Etroubles*) is 6km long. From both sides there are modern approach roads with wide curves, gradual inclines and permanent protection against snow, ensuring easy access all year. Swiss and Italian frontier posts are on the Swiss side and there is a money exchange office, restaurant, snack bar, petrol station and parking at each entrance to the tunnel.
Rates (subject to increase in 1997)

motorcycle	27 Sw F
car (according to wheelbase)	27 Sw F
car with caravan or trailer	27 Sw F
motor caravan	56.50 Sw F

KARAWANKEN, AUSTRIA/SLOVENIA
This road tunnel links Austria with Slovenia between St Jakob and Jesenice.
Rates

motorcycle	AS 90
car (not exceeding1.3 metres height)	AS 90
car with caravan or trailer	AS 135
motor caravan	AS 135

KATSCHBERG, AUSTRIA*
A two-lane carriageway 5.4 km long forming part of the motorway between Salzburg and Carinthia (Tauern autobahn).
Rates

motorcycle	AS 50
car, summer	AS 100
winter	AS 60
caravan or trailer	AS 20

LÖTSCHBERG, SWITZERLAND
Motor vehicles are transported through the Lötschberg Tunnel between Kandersteg and Goppenstein. Service

operates daily year round 0605-2305 every 30 minutes. Journey time is 15 minutes.
Rates (valid to May 1997)

motorcycle, baggage trailer	16 Sw F
car, caravan, motorcaravan (per unit)	25 Sw F
minibus (10 - 19 seats)	36 Sw F

MONT BLANC, FRANCE/ITALY
The road tunnel between Chamonix and Entrèves is 11.6 km long, and at an altitude of 1370 m. The Customs are at the Italian end. Sidelights and rear lights must be used.
Rates

motorcycle	90 FF
car (according to wheelbase)	90-185 FF
car with caravan or trailer	185 FF

PUYMORENS, FRANCE
On the N20 east of Andorra between Ax-les-Thermes and Latour.
Rates

motorcycle	18 FF
car	30 FF

RADSTADTER TAUERN, AUSTRIA*
The road tunnel is 6.5 km long and runs parallel to the Tauern railway tunnel, on the Salzburg-Carinthia route. Tolls are the same as for the Katschberg tunnel.

ST GOTTHARD, SWITZERLAND
The two-lane road tunnel is 16.3 km long running under the Gotthard Pass from Göschenen to Airolo. The tunnel is part of the national motorway network and vehicles using the road are required to display the special vignette.

SAN BERNARDINO, SWITZERLAND
The 6.6 km road tunnel runs parallel to the Pass on the N13. It is part of the national motorway network and the special vignette must be displayed.

TAUERN, AUSTRIA
Rail tunnel: Up to 47 trains a day convey vehicles between Bockstein and Mallnitz. Passengers may travel in closed cars, but only drivers in lorries and coaches. Vehicles must be loaded at least 30 minutes before departure. The journey takes 10 minutes. The Austrian Federal Railways issue a leaflet with full details and timetable.
Rates (valid to 1 June 1997)

motorcycle	AS 100
car	AS 190
caravan or trailer	AS 80

MOUNTAIN PASSES

Mountain passes are listed by country, and by road classification within each country.
The major passes are in bold type on the following tables. Dates of availability during the winter months are approximate only. The term 'intermittent closure' refers to regular snow clearance which may take two or three days.
All Swiss passes listed have emergency telephones at two-mile intervals. These may be used without charge to summon mechanical, police or medical aid.

Emergency water supplies are usually available. The Automobile Club de Suisse and the Touring Club de Suisse organise a Road Assistance Service in the Alpine regions. Foreign visitors may take advantage of this service against payment.

The RAC strongly recommends not driving over mountain passes at night and would advise inexperienced drivers either to avoid mountain passes or to drive with extreme care.

KEY TO ABBREVIATIONS

Altr	alternative	nec	necessary	S	South
Ch	winter snow chains	No	prohibited by law	Tr	treacherous
Min rad	minimum radius	NR	not recommended	u/c	unclassified road
Mod	moderate/ly	Oc	occasionally	( )	partly, in places, eg
N	North	Pic	picturesque		(narrow) = narrow in places

Road number and road, (borders) Name of Pass and height (in metres)	Min width (ft)	Max grad	Condition of Pass in winter	Recom. for caravans	Remarks
ANDORRA					
N2 L'Hospitalet to Andorra ENVALIRA 2407	20	1:8	Oc closed Nov-Apr	Yes*	*Extra care req'd. Good snow clearance, but can be closed after a heavy fall. Max height of vehicles 11'6". Highest pass in Pyrénées
AUSTRIA					
B20 St Pölten to Mariazell ANNABERG 976	13	1:8	Usually open	Yes	Pic. Light traffic.
B82 Völkermarkt to Ljubljana (Austria-Slovenia) SEEBERG 1218	16	1:8	Usually open	No	Good Altr to Loibl & Wurzen passes.
B95 Predlitz to Feldkirchen TURRACHER HOHE 1763	13	1:41/2	Usually open	No	Care req'd although no hairpins and little traffic. Road is much improved.
B99 Spittal to Radstadt KATSCHBERG 1641	**20**	**1:5**	**Usually open**	**No***	**Fairly difficult. Light traffic. *Altr motorway tunnel (toll)**
B99 Radstadt to Spittal RADSTADTER-TAUERN 1739	16	1:6	Oc closed Jan-Mar	No*	Easy pass. Mod to heavy traffic. *Use Altr motorway tunnel (toll).
B107 Bruck to Lienz GROSSGLOCKNER 2505	**16**	**1:8**	**Closed late Oct-early May**	**No***	**Toll. *Only powerful caravan units, preferably S-N. Hairpin bends, exceptional views. Seasonal traffic. Tunnel at summit.**
B109 Villach to Kranjska Gora (Austria-Slovenia) WURZEN 1073	13	1:51/2	Usually open	No*	Steep road, fairly difficult. Heavy traffic summer weekends. *Caravans prohibited. NR for other vehicles.
B110/SS52B Kötschach-Mauthen to Tolmezzo (Austria-Italy) PLOCKEN 1362	16	1:7	Oc closed Dec-Apr	No*	Heavy traffic summer weekends – delays likely at frontier. *Some sections reconstructed so pass just negotiable for caravans. Extra care.
138 Windischgarsten to Liezen PYHRN 945	**13**	**1:10**	**Usually open**	**Yes**	**Several hairpins. Altr road tunnel (toll).**

Road number and road, (borders), Name of Pass and height (in metres)	Min width (ft)	Max grad	Condition of Pass in winter	Recom. for caravans	Remarks
B145 Bad Ischl to Bad Aussee POTSCHEN 972	23	1:11	**Usually open**	Yes	**Views of the Dachstein. Mod to heavy traffic.**
B161 Kitzbühel to Mittersill THURN 1274	16	1:12	**Usually open**	Yes	**Scenic. Mod to heavy traffic.**
B165 Zell am Ziller to Mittersill GERLOS PLATTE 1628	13	1:12	Usually open	No*	Mod to heavy traffic. Toll road. *Caravans prohibited.
B181/B307 Jenbach to Tegernsee (Austria-Germany) AACHEN 941	19	1:7	Usually open*	No	Pic. Mod to heavy traffic. *Closed in winter to lorries with trailers, and truck tractors.
B182/SS12 Innsbruck to Bolzano (Austria-Italy) BRENNER 1374	20	1:7	**Usually open**	No*	**Pic. Lowest, busiest transalpine pass. Ch sometimes. *Use Altr route via autobahn (toll). Pass is closed to vehicles towing.**
B186/SS44B Otz to Merano (Austria-Italy) TIMMELSJOCH 2509	12	1:7	Closed early Oct-late June	No*	Toll. No minibuses. NR. *The pass is **only** open to private cars without trailers.
B188 Bludenz to Landeck SILVRETTA/BIELERHOHE 2032	16	1:9	Closed late Oct-early June	No*	Toll. Light traffic. *Caravans prohibited. 32 hairpin bends.
B197 Feldkirch to Innsbruck ARLBERG 1793	20	1:71/2	**Oc closed Dec-Apr**	No*	**Pic. Fairly easy, heavy traffic. *Closed to vehicles towing. Altr road tunnel (toll).**
B198 Stuben to Reutte FLEXEN 1773	18	1:10	Usually open*	No	Fine views, light traffic. *The road N of the pass from Lech-Warth is usually closed Nov-April through danger of avalanches.
B200 Egg to Warth HOCHTANNBERG 1679	13	1:7	Oc closed late Dec-Mar	No	Road has been reconstructed.
B306 Gloggnitz to Mürzzuschlag SEMMERING 985	20	1:16	Usually open	Yes	Fine views. Heavy traffic. Several hairpin bends.
B314 Imst to Reutte FERN 1210	20	1:10	**Usually open**	Yes	**Easy pass. Heavy traffic. Extra care req'd after rain.**
B315/SS40 Landeck to Malles (Austria-Italy) RESIA 1504	20	1:10	**Usually open**	Yes	**Mod to heavy traffic. Pic Altr to the Brenner Pass.**

FRANCE

N5 Morez to Genève FAUCILLE 1323	16	1:10	**Usually open**	No*	***Experience necessary. Altr via Nyon-Genève. View of Mt Blanc.**
N6 Chambéry to Torino MT CENIS 2083	16	1:8	**Closed early Nov-mid May**	Yes	**Heavy summer traffic, easy to drive. Poor surface. Altr road tunnel (toll).**
N20 Toulouse to Bourg-Madame PUYMORENS 1915	18	1:10	**Oc closed Nov-Apr**	Yes	**Altr road tunnel (toll). Not suitable for night driving. Max height of vehicles 11'6"**
N75 Grenoble to Sisteron CROIX-HAUTE 1176	18	1:14	**Usually open**	Yes	**Hairpin bends. Open to all vehicles.**
N85 Grenoble to Gap (Route des Alpes) BAYARD 1248	20	1:7	**Usually open**	No*	**Fairly easy, but steep S side and several hairpins. *Just negotiable for caravans N-S. Altr route via N75**

Road number and road, (borders), Name of Pass and height (in metres)	Min width (ft)	Max grad	Condition of Pass in winter	Recom. for caravans	Remarks
N90/SS26 Bourg-St-Maurice to Aosta (France-Italy) PETIT ST BERNARD 2188	16	1:12	Closed mid Oct-mid June	No	Light traffic. Pic. No vehicles over 15 tons. Unguarded edges at summit
N91 Briançon to Vizille LAUTARET/ALTARETO 2058	14	1:8	Oc closed Dec-Mar	Yes	Unguarded edges. NR buses. Heavy summer traffic. Magnificent scenery.
N94/SS24 Briançon to Torino (France-Italy) MONTGENEVRE 1850	16	1:11	Usually open	Yes	Open all year. Altr Mt Cenis. Heavy traffic. Pic. Ch.
N204/SS20 La Giandola to Borgo San Dalmazzo (France-Italy) COL DE TENDE 1321	18	1:11	Usually open	Yes*	Heavy summer traffic. Tunnel at summit. Many well-engineered hairpin bends. *Caravans prohibited in winter. Closed 2100-0600 hrs.
N506 Chamonix to Martigny COL DES MONTETS 1461	10	1:8	Oc closed Dec- early Apr	Yes*	*Small caravans only. Narrow and rough surface in places.
D64 Jausiers to St Etienne-de-Tinée RESTEFOND 2802	10	1:9	Closed Oct-June	No	The highest pass in the Alps. Narrow, rough unguarded ascent. Many hairpin bends. Extra care req'd.
D118 Carcassonne to Mont-Louis QUILLANNE 1714	16	1:12	Oc closed Nov-Mar	Yes	Easy drive.
D465 St Maurice-sur-Moselle to Belfort BALLON D'ALSACE 1178	13	1:9	Oc closed Dec-end Mar	Yes*	Fairly easy, but many bends. *Care req'd.
D618 Arreau to Bagnères-de-Luchon PEYRESOURDE 1563	13	1:10	Usually open	No	Fairly easy to drive, but several hairpins. (Narrow) .
D618 St-Girons to Tarascon-sur-Ariège PORT 1249	14	1:10	Oc closed Nov-Mar	Yes*	Pic, narrow road. *NR large caravans.
D900/SS21 Barcelonnette to Cúneo (France-Italy) LARCHE/ARGENTERA 1994	10	1:12	Oc closed Dec-Mar	Yes	Light traffic, easy to drive. Narrow/rough on ascent.
D902 St Michel-de-Maurienne to Lautaret Saddle GALIBIER 2645	10	1:8	Closed Oct-June	No	Weekend heavy traffic. Numerous hairpin bends, unguarded edges. Tunnel under summit is closed
D902 Lanslebourg to Bourg-St-MauriceI L'Iseran 2770	13	1:9	Closed mid Oct-late June	No	Care req'd on northern approach – unlit tunnels.
D902 Briançon to Guillestre IZOARD 2361	16	1:8	Closed late Oct-mid June	No	Winter avalanches. Narrow/winding road. Care req'd near Guillestre – unlit tunnels.
D902 Barcelonnette to Guillestre VARS 2111	16	1:10	Oc closed Dec-Mar	No	Many hairpins and steep sections. NR buses.
D908 Barcelonnette to Entrevaux ALLOS 2250	13	1:10	Closed early Nov-early June	No	Pic, narrow road mostly unguarded. NR inexperienced drivers. Max width 5'11".
D909 Annecy to Chamonix ARAVIS 1498	13	1:11	Oc closed Dec-Mar	No	Pic. Fairly easy. NR buses.
D918 Arreau to Luz-St-Sauveur ASPIN 1489	13	1:8	Closed Dec-April	Yes	Pic.
D918 Laruns to Argelès-Gazost AUBISQUE 1710	11	1:10	Closed mid Oct-June	No	Pic but Tr. Rough and narrow in parts. Unguarded edges with a steep drop.

Road number and road, (borders), Name of Pass and height (in metres)	Min width (ft)	Max grad	Condition of Pass in winter	Recom. for caravans	Remarks
D918 Luz-St-Sauveur to Arreau TOURMALET 2115	14	1:8	Closed Oct-mid June	No	Highest pass in French Pyrénées. NR buses: sufficiently guarded.
D934/C136 Pau to Huesca (France-Spain) POURTALET 1792	11	1:10	Closed late Oct-early June	No	Fairly easy, unguarded road. Narrow in places.
D2202 Barcelonnette to Nice CAYOLLE 2327	13	1:10	Closed early Nov-early June	No	Fairly difficult. Sharp hairpin bends, unfenced in places with steep drops. Much single-track road.

GERMANY

B307/B181 Tegernsee to Jenbach (Germany-Austria) AACHEN 941	19	1:7	Usually open*	No	Pic. Mod to heavy traffic. *Closed in winter to lorries with trailers, and truck tractors.

ITALY

SS12/B182 Bolzano to Innsbruck (Italy-Austria) BRENNER 1374	**20**	**1:7**	**Usually open**	**No***	**Pic. Lowest, busiest transalpine pass. Ch sometimes. *Use altr route via autobahn (toll). Pass is closed to vehicles towing.**
SS20/N204 Borgo San Dalmazzo to La Giandola (Italy-France) COL DE TENDE 1321	**18**	**1:11**	**Usually open**	**Yes***	**Heavy summer traffic. Tunnel at summit. Many well-engineered hairpin bends. *Caravans prohibited in winter. Closed 2100-0600 hrs.**
SS21/D900 Cúneo to Barcelonnette (Italy-France) ARGENTERA/LARCHE 1994	10	1:12	Oc closed Dec-Mar	Yes	Light traffic, easy to drive. Narrow/rough on ascent, better surface on descent.
SS23 Cesana Torinese to Torino SESTRIERE 2033	16	1:10	Usually open	Yes*	Access to winter sports resort. Fine scenery. Fairly easy pass. *Care req'd.
SS24/N94 Torino to Briançon (Italy-France) MONTGENEVRE 1850	**16**	**1:11**	**Usually open**	**Yes**	**Open all year. Altr Mt Cenis. Heavy traffic Pic. Ch.**
SS26/N90 Aosta to Bourg-St-Maurice (Italy-France) PETIT ST BERNARD 2188	**16**	**1:12**	**Closed mid Oct-mid June**	**No**	**Light traffic. Pic. No vehicles over 15 tons. Unguarded edges at summit.**
SS27/A21 Aosta to Martigny (Italy-Switzerland) GREAT ST BERNARD 2473	**16**	**1:10**	**Closed Oct-June**	**No***	***Pass closed to vehicles towing – use Altr toll tunnel. Fairly easy – care req'd over summit. Ch sometimes req'd on approach roads, but not permitted through tunnel.**
SS36 Chiavenna to Splügen (Italy-Switzerland) SPLUGEN 2113	**10**	**1:7½**	**Closed early Nov-June**	**No**	**Pic. Many hairpin bends, not well guarded. Max height of vehicles 9'2". Max width 7'6".**
SS38 Bormio to Spondigna STELVIO 2757	**13**	**1:8**	**Closed Oct-late June**	**No**	**Many hairpins, very scenic. No vehicles over 30ft in length.**
SS38 Bormio to Santa Maria (Italy-Switzerland) UMBRAIL 2501	14	1:11	Closed early Nov-early June	No	Mod difficult. No trailers. No vehicles over 7'6" wide
SS39 Edolo to Tresenda APRICA 1176	13	1:11	Usually open	Yes	Pic. Ch nec at times.
SS40/B315 Malles to Landeck (Italy-Austria) RESIA 1504	**20**	**1:10**	**Usually open**	**Yes**	**Mod to heavy traffic. Pic Altr to the Brenner Pass.**
SS42 Bolzano to Fondo MENDOLA 1363	16	1:8	Usually open	Yes	Light traffic. Superb views.

Road number and road, (borders), Name of Pass and height (in metres)	Min width (ft)	Max grad	Condition of Pass in winter	Recom. for caravans	Remarks
SS42 Edolo to Bolzano TONALE 1883	16	1:8	Usually open	Yes	Easy drive.
SS44 Merano to Vipiteno MONTE GIOVO 2094	13	1:8	Closed Nov-May	No*	Scenic. Hairpin bends. *Caravans prohibited.
SS44B/B186 Merano to Otz (Italy-Austria) TIMMELSJOCH 2509	12	1:7	Closed early Oct-late June	No*	Toll. No minibuses. NR. *The pass is only open to private cars without trailers.
SS46 Rovereto to Vicenza FUGAZZE 1159	10	1:7	Usually open	No	Hairpin bends. Narrow on N side; extra care req'd.
SS48 Ora to Cortina FALZAREGO 2117	16	1:12	Oc closed Dec-Apr	No*	Many hairpins. *Only just suitable for powerful cars.
SS48 Arabba to Canazei PORDOI 2239	16	1:10	Oc closed Dec-Apr	No	Excellent views of the Dolomites. Hairpin bends.
SS48 Cortina to Auronzo TRE CROCI 1809	16	1:9	Oc closed Dec-Mar	Yes	Very easy drive. Pic.
SS50 Predazzo to Primiero ROLLE 1970	16	1:11	Oc closed Dec-Mar	Yes*	Beautiful scenery. *Not easy.
SS52 Pieve di Cadore to Piani MAURIA 1298	16	1:14	Usually open	Yes	Winding road.
SS52B/B110 Tolmezzo to Kötschach Mauthen (Italy-Austria) PLOCKEN 1362	16	1:7	Oc closed Dec-Apr	No*	Heavy traffic summer weekends – delays likely at frontier. *Some sections reconstructed so pass just negotiable for caravans. Extra care req'd.
SS239 Tione di Trento to Dimaro CAMPIGLIO 1682	-	1:8½	Oc closed Dec-Mar	Yes	Easy pass. Pic.
SS241 Cortina to Bolzano COSTALUNGA 1753	16	1:7	Oc closed Dec-Apr	No*	Many blind bends (difficult). Caravans proohibited.
SS242 Ortisei to Canazei SELLA 2240	16	1:9	Oc closed late Nov-early June	No	Pic. Winding roads. Good views of the Dolomites.
SS243 Selva to Corvara GARDENA 2121	16	1:8	Oc closed Dec-June	No	Pic. Very winding on descent.
SS244 Corvara to Arabba CAMPOLONGO 1875	16	1:8	Oc closed Dec-Mar	Yes	Pic. Winding, but easy.
SS300 Bormio to Ponte di Legno GAVIA 2621	14	1:5½	Closed Oct-July	No	Beautiful rocky scenery. Experienced drivers only. Max width 5'11".

SPAIN

NIII Tarancon to Requena CONTRERAS 890	22	1:14	Open	Yes	Min rad bends 32'. Well protected. Using NIII avoids the pass.
NVI Madrid to La Coruña GUADARRAMA 1511	26	1:8	Intermittent closure	Yes	Min rad turning 82'. Altr road tunnel on A6 motorway.
N111 Logroño to Donostia/San Sebastián LIZARRAGA 1031	17½	1:14	Open	Yes	Min rad turning 32'.

Road number and road, (borders), Name of Pass and height (in metres)	Min width (ft)	Max grad	Condition of Pass in winter	Recom. for caravans	Remarks
N152 Barcelona to Puigcerdà TOSAS 1800	16	1:10	Usually open	Yes*	Fairly straightforward but some sharp bends and a few unguarded edges. *Negotiable for caravans with extra care.
N240 Pamplona to Donostia/San Sebastián AZPIROZ 616	19	1:10	Usually open	Yes	Double bends. Min rad bends 42'.
N240 Gasteiz/Vitoria to Bilbao BARAZAR 604	21	1:11	Open	Yes*	Min rad bends 39'. *Approach roads require care when towing.
N330/N134 Huesca to Pau SOMPORT 1632	12	1:10	Usually open	Yes	Easy drive. Usual route across Pyrénées. Narrow and unguarded in parts.
N400 Tarancon to Cuenca CABREJAS 1166	16	1:7	Usually open	Yes	
N525 Zamora to Orense CANDA 1260	23	1:8	Intermittent closure	Yes	Min rad turning 49'. Easy road.
N601 Madrid to Segovia NAVACERRADA 1860	19 1/2	1:11	Usually open	No	Some tricky hairpin bends.
N623 Burgos to Santander CARRALES 1020	22	1:16 1/2	Open*	No*	*Other passes on this road NR for caravans & closed in winter.
C135 Pamplona to St-Jean-Pied-de-Port IBANETA 1057	13	1:10	Usually open	Yes*	Pic. *Drive with care.
C136/D934 Huesca to Pau (Spain-France) POURTALET 1792	11	1:10	Closed late Oct-early June	No	Fairly easy, unguarded road. Narrow in places.
C142 Esterri d'Aneu to Viella BONAIGUA 2072	14	1:12	Closed Nov-Apr	No	Narrow road, hairpin bends. Dangerous. Altr Viella road tunnel is open in winter.

SWITZERLAND

N2 Andermatt to Bellinzona ST GOTTHARD 2108	20	1:10	Closed mid Oct-early June	Yes*	No vehicles over 8'2 1/2" wide or 11'9" high. Many hairpins and heavy summer traffic. *Altr motorway tunnel is better – Swiss tax charged.
N8 (N4) Meiringen to Lucerne BRUNIG 1007	20	1:12	Usually open	Yes	No vehicles over 8'2 1/2" wide. Ch sometimes. Heavy traffic at weekends.
N9 Brig to Domodossola SIMPLON 2005	23	1:9	Oc closed Nov-Apr	Yes	Max width 8'2". An easy, reconstructed road.
N13 Chur to Bellinzona SAN BERNARDINO 2006	3	1:10	Closed Oct-late June	No*	Easy approach roads, but narrow, winding summit. *Use motorway tunnel Altr – Swiss tax charged. Max width 7'6".
A3 Tiefencastel to Silvaplana JULIER 2284	13	1:7 1/2	Usually open	Yes*	*Easier N-S. Max width 8'2 1/2". Altr rail tunnel Tiefencastelsamedan.
A3 Chiavenna to Silvaplana MALOJA 1815	13	1:11	Usually open	Yes*	Many hairpin bends on descent. No trailers. *Easier on descent than ascent. Just negotiable. Max width 8'2 1/2" – all vehicles.
A6 Gletsch to Innertkirchen GRIMSEL 2165	16	1:10	Closed mid Oct-late June	No	No vehicles over 7'6" wide. Many hairpins, seasonal traffic. Max weight trailers 2 1/2 tons.

Road number and road, (borders), Name of Pass and height (in metres)	Min width (ft)	Max grad	Condition of Pass in winter	Recom. for caravans	Remarks
A11 Aigle to Saanen COL DES MOSSES 1445	13	1:12	Usually open	Yes	Pic. No coaches. Ch req'd in winter. Max width 7'6".
A11 Innertkirchen to Wassen SUSTEN 2224	0	1:11	Closed late Oct-early June	Yes*	Well engineered, scenic, heavy traffic. Long delays at 3mile single-track section. No vehicles over 8'2½" wide. *Extra care req'd.
A17 Altdorf to Glarus KLAUSEN 194	16	1:11	Usually closed late Oct-early June	No*	No vehicles over 7'6" wide. Caravans prohibited.
A19 Andermatt to Brig FURKA 2431	**13**	**1:10**	**Closed Oct-June**	**No**	**Seasonal traffic. No vehicles over 7'6" wide. Many hairpin bends. Altr rail tunnel.**
A19 Andermatt to Disentis OBERALP 2044	16	1:10	Closed early Nov-late May	No*	Max width 7'6". Road improved but still many hairpins. *Pass just negotiable for caravans, extra care req'd. Altr rail tunnel available in winter.
A21/SS27 Martigny to Aosta (Switzerland-Italy) GREAT ST BERNARD 2473	**16**	**1:10**	**Closed Oct-June**	**No***	***Pass closed to vehicles towing – use Altr toll tunnel. Fairly easy – care req'd over summit. Ch sometimes req'd on approach roads, but not permitted through tunnel.**
A28 Landquart to Susch FLUELA 2383	16	1:8	Oc closed Nov-May	Yes*	Light traffic, easy drive. No vehicles over 7'6" wide, 11'2" high. *Extra care req'd. Closed at night.
A28 Zernez to Santa Maria OFEN 2149	12	1:8	Usually open	Yes	No vehicles over 7'6" wide. Ch sometimes req'd.
A29 Celerina to Tirano BERNINA 2330	16	1:8	Oc closed late Dec-Mar*	No	Pic, narrow and winding on S side. Care needed. Max width 7'6". *Closed at night.
A189 Bulle to Spiez JAUN 1509	13	1:10	Usually open	No	Very attractive scenery. No vehicles over 7'6" wide.
A203 Martigny to Chamonix FORCLAZ 1527	16	1:12	Usually open	Yes*	No vehicles over 8'2½" wide. No trailers over 5 tons. *Just negotiable.
A461 Disentis to Biasca LUKMANIER 1916	16	1:11	Closed early Nov-late May	Yes	Rebuilt, modern road. Max width 7'6".
(SS36) Splügen to Chiavenna (Switzerland-Italy) SPLUGEN 2113	**10**	**1:7½**	**Closed early Nov-June**	**No**	**Pic. Many hairpin bends, not well guarded. Max height of vehicles 9'2". Max width of vehicles 7'6"**
(SS38) Santa Maria to Bormio (Switzerland-Italy) UMBRAIL 2501	14	1:11	Closed early Nov-early June	No	Mod difficult. No trailers. No vehicles over 7'6" wide.
u/c Tiefencastel to La Punt (via Bergün) ALBULA 2315	12	1:10	Closed early Nov-early June	No	Light traffic, sharp bends. No lorries and trailers. Altr rail tunnel. Max width 7'6".
u/c Aigle to Saanen (via Gstaad) COL DU PILLON 1546	13	1:11	Oc closed Jan-Feb	Yes	No vehicles over 7'6" wide. Ch sometimes req'd.
u/c Brig to Airolo (via Bedretto) NUFENEN 2478	13	1:10	Closed mid Oct-mid June	No*	Approach roads narrow, but road over pass good. *Just negotiable to light caravans (less than 1½ tons). Max width 7'6".

Escape

At the RAC we can release you from
the worries of motoring

But did you know that we can also
give you invaluable peace of mind
when you go on holiday,

Or arrange your hotel bookings,

Or even organise your entire
holiday, all over the phone?

RAC Travel Insurance   0800 550 055

RAC Hotel Reservations   0345 056 042

RAC Holiday Reservations   0161 480 4810

Call us

EMERGENCIES

WHAT TO DO IF YOU ARE INVOLVED IN AN ACCIDENT

The following represents the procedure that should be taken if you are involved in an accident while abroad.

1. Immediately report the accident to the police. This is compulsory in the event of personal injuries.

2. Give your name and address, and that of your insurance company, to the other party and produce your International Motor Insurance Certificate (Green Card) if required.

3. Accidents involving a third party must be reported at once to the appropriate insurance bureau of the country concerned, the details of which appear on the Green Card. Also immediately notify your own insurance company.

4. In no circumstances should you make any statement or sign any document without the advice of a lawyer or official of the local automobile club.

5. Should a camera be available, take photographs of the post-accident positions of the vehicles, marks on the road, etc, from as many angles as possible.

6. If it is essential to move the vehicles, first mark the positions of their wheels with chalk on the road.

7. Make a rough sketch showing position of the vehicles both before and at the time of the accident, indicating the direction in which you were travelling.

8. Be sure that you take the following particulars:
    a. Make and registration number of the other vehicle and whether right- or left-hand drive.
    b. Full name, address and occupation of the driver of the other vehicle and number, etc, of his driving licence, as well as full name, address and occupation of the owner if not the driver.
    c. Other party's insurance company details, policy number and Green Card number.
    d. Full names, addresses and occupations of independent witnesses.
    e. Date, time and exact place of accident.
    f. Speeds of your own and other vehicle.
    g. Signals given by yourself and other driver.
    h. Condition of brakes, tyres, lights (front and rear) of both vehicles.
    i. Weather and road conditions.
    j. Names and addresses of persons injured and nature of injuries.
    k. Damage to your own and other vehicle.
    l. Address of police to whom accident reported.

9. RAC Members should seek advice from the local FIA or AIT Club, or from RAC European Support, ☎ 0181-686 0088. Addresses and telephone numbers of the FIA and AIT clubs are given for each country in the Europe by Country section of this guide.

10. Purchasers of RAC European Motoring Assistance should also consult their Assistance Book. Reflex Europe Members should consult 'Your Guide to Membership and How to Obtain Assistance'.

In **Belgium**, unless people have been injured, you must, if possible, move your vehicle to the side and off the road so that traffic is not obstructed.

In **France**, if an accident involving personal injury or substantial damage occurs in a town, get a policeman (*agent de police*) to make a report. On country roads send for a *gendarme*. In accidents involving damage only, ask for the services of a *huissier* from a neighbouring town or village. A *huissier* is a court official who acts partly as an assessor and partly as a bailiff. The party requesting his services is responsible for the fee for drawing up a report of the accident.

WHAT TO DO IF YOU BREAK DOWN

If you have taken out RAC European Motoring Assistance you should check the break-down section of your Assistance Book. If you are an RAC Reflex Europe Member, you should check 'Your Guide to Membership and How to Obtain Assistance'.

To obtain assistance if you have not purchased any of the above services, contact the nearest garage or agent for your make of car. The police often have lists of 24-hour garages if you cannot find one which is open. On motorways, including service areas, you must use the emergency telephone system, which will normally connect you to the police or company operating the motorway.

KEEPING IN CONTACT

EMERGENCY RADIO MESSAGES

Members touring abroad can be informed of serious illness in the family through the courtesy of the BBC. In an emergency, contact RAC Travel Information at Croydon, ☎ 0345 333 222, and if the following information is provided, arrangements will be made for a message to be transmitted in the relevant country:

1. Full name and home address of person for whom message is intended.
2. Their possible whereabouts.
3. Registration number and description of vehicle.
4. Full name and address of the person ill and relationship.
5. Name, home address and telephone number of the doctor attending or of hospital.
6. Reason for message (eg mother seriously ill).
7. Full name, address and telephone number of person sending the message.

If the use of this service is foreseen, a Member should leave details of the day to day itinerary.

These emergency messages can be broadcast in most European countries.

The BBC cannot broadcast a notification of death in the family and only very important messages will be accepted.

RADIO FREQUENCIES

BBC WORLD SERVICE
The BBC World Service broadcasts in English 24 hours each day. World News is broadcast on the hour.

Radio frequencies in kHz

	06.00–08.30	08.30–17.00	17.00–23.30
Albania	12095, 9410, 6180	17640, 15070, 12095	15070, 12095, 9410, 6180
Austria	15575, 9410, 6195	15070, 12095	12095, 9410, 6195
Belgium	15575, 9410, 648	12095, 9750, 648	12095, 9410, 6195, 648
Bulgaria	15070, 12095, 9410	17640, 15070, 9660	15070, 12095, 9410
CIS/ Baltic States	12095, 9410	15070, 12095, 17640	15070, 12095, 6180
Czech Republic and Slovakia	15575, 9410, 6195, 3955	15070, 12095	12095, 9410, 6195, 3955
Denmark	6195, 3955	12095, 9410	12095, 6195, 3955, 6180
Finland	12095, 9410	15070, 12095	15070, 12095, 9410
France (North)	12095, 6195, 648	12095, 9410, 648	12095, 9410, 6195, 648
France (South)	9410, 6195,	15070, 12095, 9410	12095, 9410, 6195
Germany (North East)	15575, 9410, 6195	15070, 12095	12095, 9410, 6195
Germany (North West)	15575, 9410, 648	12095, 9750, 648	12095, 9410, 6195
Germany (South)	15575, 9410, 6195	15070, 12095	12095, 9410, 6195

Radio Frequencies

	06.00–08.30	08.30–17.00	17.00–23.30
Gibraltar	9410, 6195	15070, 12095	15070, 12095, 9410, 6195
Greece	15070, 12095, 9410, 1323	17640, 15070, 9660, 1323	15070, 12095, 9410, 1323
Hungary	15070, 12095, 9410	15070, 12095	12095, 9410, 6195
Ireland	15575, 9410, 648	12095, 9750, 648	12095, 9410, 6195
Italy (North)	9410, 6195	15070, 12095	12095, 9410, 6195
Italy (South)	12095, 9410	17640, 15070, 12095	15070, 12095, 9410
Luxembourg	15575, 9410, 648	12095, 648	12095, 9410, 6195
Malta	12095, 9410	17640, 15070, 12095	15070, 12095, 9410
Netherlands	15575, 9410, 648, 3955	12095, 9750, 648	12095, 9410, 6195, 648, 3955
Norway (North)	12095, 9410	15070, 12095, 9410	15070, 12095, 9410
Norway (South)	9410, 6195, 3955	12095, 9410	9410, 6195, 3955
Poland	15575, 9410, 6195, 3955	15070, 12095	12095, 9410, 6195, 3955
Portugal	9410, 6195, 3955	15070, 12095, 9410	15070, 12095, 9410, 6195
Romania	15070, 12095, 9410	17640, 15070, 12095	15070, 12095, 9410
Serbia	15070, 6180, 1323	17640, 15070	15070, 12095, 6180
Slovenia	15575, 12095, 9410	15070, 12095	15070, 12095, 9410
Spain	9410, 6195, 3955	15070, 12095, 9410	15070, 12095, 9410, 6195
Sweden	12095, 9410, 6195, 3955	15070, 12095, 9410	15070, 12095, 9410, 6195, 3955
Switzerland	15575, 9410, 6195, 3955	15070, 12095	12095, 9410, 6195, 3955
Turkey	15070, 6180, 1323	17640, 15070, 1323	15070, 12095, 6180, 1323
(Former) Yugoslavia	15070, 12095, 9410	17640, 15070, 9660	15070, 12095, 9410

Full programme and frequency details can be obtained from BBC World Service Publicity, PO Box 76, Bush House, Strand, London, WC2B 4PH.
Times shown are local.
Of the BBC's domestic services, Radio 1 on 275/285m (1089/1053kHz) medium wave, Radio 4 on 1515m (198kHz) long wave, and Radio 5 on 433/330m (693/909kHz) medium wave, are widely audible in north-west Europe.
Frequencies may vary between summer and winter. Short wave reception varies according to location and all frequencies should be tried on air to find the best one. Lower frequencies generally give best results at night, higher ones during the day.

TELEPHONING HOME

To call the UK from a European country, the complete number you will need to dial comprises: **Access code + Country code + UK area (STD) code (leaving out the initial 0) + local number.**

In Europe, dialling tones may differ from those in Britain. Dial steadily without pauses, unless it is necessary to wait for a second dialling tone (where indicated by an asterisk in the following pages). Connection can take up to one minute; a persistent tone or recorded announcement means that your call has not gone through, and you should try again.

INTERNATIONAL TELEPHONE CODES

The following dialling codes are used for direct dialling from one European country to another. The Access code is used for the country from which the call is being made, and the Country code for the country to which the call is going. For example, to call Spain from Finland, dial 990 34 followed by the internal area code.

	Access code	Country code			Access code	Country code
Andorra	00	33 628		Great Britain	00	44
Austria	00	43		Greece	00	30
Belgium	00 or 00*	32		Hungary	00*	36
Bulgaria	00	359		Italy	00	39
CIS	-	7		Latvia	-	371
(Azerbaijan	-	994)		Lithuania	-	370
(Moldava	-	373)		Luxembourg	00	352
Croatia	99	38		Netherlands	00	31
Cyprus	00	357		Norway	095	47
Czech Republic ans Slovakia	00	42		Portugal	00	351
Denmark	00	45		Romania	-	40
Estonia	-	372		Slovenia	00	386
Finland	990	358		Spain	07*	34
France	00	33		Sweden	009	46
Germany	00	49		Switzerland	00	41
Gibraltar	00	350		Turkey	00	90

* Await a second tone at this stage

HOW TO SET UP A CALL

AUSTRIA
Lift receiver, check for dial tone. Insert at least 15 Schillings or phonecard, dial. A signal indicates when to insert more money. Fully unused coins refunded Coins accepted: 1, 5, 10, 20 Sch. Phonecards: 50, 100 Sch. Local international operator: 09. UK Direct operator: 022 903 044. Reverse charge calls available. BT Chargecard Direct number 022 903 044.

BELGIUM
Lift receiver, check for dial tone. Insert money or 'Telecard', dial. A signal indicates when to insert more money or 'Telecard'. Fully unused coins refunded. Coins accepted: 20 BF. Phonecards: 200, 1,000 BF 'Telecards' (available from railway stations, post offices, newsagents and tobacconists). UK Direct operator 0800 100 44. Reverse charge calls available.

When you're abroad, you can use your BT Chargecard to call from more than 80 countries, thanks to the BT Direct service.

A BT Chargecard is available FREE on 0800 800 893

(Belgium cont.)
BT Chargecard Direct number 0800 100 44. Cheap rate: Mon-Sat 2000-0800, all day Sunday.

CYPRUS

Lift receiver, check for dial tone. Insert at least 10 cents or 'Telecard', dial. A signal indicates when to insert more money. Fully unused coins refunded. Coins accepted: 2, 5, 10, 20c. Phonecards: 2, 5, 10 Cyprus pound. 'Telecards' (available from banks, post offices and some kiosks). Local international operator: 198. UK Direct operator: 080 900 44. Reverse charge calls available. BT Chargecard Direct number 080 900 44 (not available from the Turkish sector).

DENMARK

Lift receiver, check for dial tone. Insert at least 1 Kr or phonecard, dial. A signal indicates when to insert more money. Fully unused coins refunded. Coins accepted: 1, 5, 10, 20 Kr. Phonecards: available from Telecom shops ('Telebutik'). Local international operator: 115. UK Direct operator: 80 01 04 44. Reverse charge calls available. BT Chargecard Direct number 80 01 04 44.

FINLAND

Lift receiver, check for dial tone. Insert 1 FIM, dial. Coins accepted: 1, 5 Mk. Phonecards: accepted at some phones. UK Direct operator: 9800 1 0440. BT Chargecard Direct number 9800 1 0440.

FRANCE

Lift receiver, check for dial tone. Insert money or 'Télécarte', dial. A signal indicates when to insert more money. Fully unused coins refunded. Coins accepted: 1, 5, 10F. Phonecards: 40, 96F 'Télécartes' (available from post offices, SNCF counters, tobacconists and France Telecom commercial agencies). Local international operator: 00 33 44. UK Direct operator: 0800 99 00 44. Reverse charge calls available. Cheap rate: Mon-Fri 2130-0800, Sat 1400-2400, all day Sunday. BT Chargecard Direct number 0800 99 02 44.
From 18 October 1996 most French telephone numbers were given an additional digit, either '2', '3', '4' or '5' in front of the old eight digits. (Paris already had a '1' in front.) Each quadrant of France (excluding Paris) now takes a different number: North West '2' eg Nantes; North East '3' eg Calais; South East '4' eg Nice; South West '5' eg Bordeaux.

GERMANY

Lift receiver, check for dial tone. Insert 2 DM or phonecard, dial. A signal indicates when to insert more money. Coins accepted: 10pf; 1, 5 DM. Phonecards: available from post offices and tobacconists. Local international operator: 01114 (available only from former East Germany). UK Direct operator: 0130 80 0044 (available only from former West Germany). Reverse charge calls available. Cheap rate: Mon-Fri 1800-0800, all weekend. BT Chargecard Direct number 0130 80 0044.

GREECE

Lift receiver, check for dial tone. Insert at least 10 Drachmas, dial. A red light indicates when to insert more money. Fully unused coins refunded. Coins accepted: 10 Dr. Local international operator: 161. Reverse charge calls only via local international operator. Cheap rate: Mon-Fri 1500-1700 & 2200-0900, Sat after 1500, all day Sunday. BT Chargecard Direct number 00 800 4411.

IRELAND

Lift receiver, check for dial tone. Insert at least 50p or phonecard, dial. A signal indicates when to insert more money. Fully unused coins refunded. Coins accepted: 5, 10, 20, 50p. Phonecards: IR £2, £3.50, £8, £16. Local international operator: 114 Dublin; 10 elsewhere. UK Direct operator: 1 800 55 0044. Reverse charge calls only via local international operator. Cheap rate: Mon-Fri 1800-0800, all weekend. BT Chargecard Direct number 1 800 550044.

ITALY

Lift receiver, check for dial tone. Insert at least 2,000 Lira, tokens or phonecard, dial. A signal indicates when to insert more money, tokens or phonecard. Press button to recover fully unused coins or tokens. Coins accepted: 100, 200, 500L coins or tokens ('gettoni'). Phonecards: 5,000, 10,000L (available from newsagents, post offices and some railway stations).

You will also be able to direct dial from a steadily increasing number of countries back to the UK. You can already do so from France.

A BT Chargecard is available FREE on 0800 800 893

Local international operator: 15, UK Direct operator: 172 0044. Reverse charge calls available. Cheap rate: Mon-Sat 2200-0800, all day Sunday. BT Chargecard Direct number 15.

LUXEMBOURG

Lift receiver, insert 5 Francs. Check for dial tone, dial. Coins accepted: 1, 5, 20F (Lux/Belgian). Local international operator: 0010. UK Direct operator: 0800 0044. Reverse charge calls available. BT Chargecard Direct number 0800 0044.

NETHERLANDS

Lift receiver, insert at least two 25c coins or phonecard. Check for dial tone, dial. A signal indicates when to insert more money or phonecard. Fully unused coins will be refunded.
Coins accepted: 25c; 1, 2.5G. Phonecards: 5, 10, 25, 40 DF (available from railway stations, post offices, tourist offices and outlets displaying the cardphone sign). Local international operator: 06*0410. UK Direct operator: 06*022 9944. Reverse charge calls available. Cheap rate: Mon-Fri 2000-0600, all weekend. BT Chargecard Direct number 06 0410.

NORWAY

Lift receiver, check for dial tone. Insert at least 5 Kr or phonecard, dial. A signal indicates when to insert more money. Fully unused coins refunded.
Phonecards: 24, 100 Kr. Local international operator: 0115. UK Direct operator: 800 19 044. Reverse charge calls available. Cheap rate: Daily 2200-0800. BT Chargecard Direct number 800 19 044.

PORTUGAL

Lift receiver, check for dial tone. Insert at least four 50 Escudos or phonecard, dial. A signal indicates when to insert more money. Fully unused coins refunded.
Phonecards: 500, 1,200 Esc. (available from post offices, tobacconists and telephone bureaux). Local international operator: 098 or 099. UK Direct operator: 0505 00 44. Reverse charge calls available. BT Chargecard Direct number 0505 00 44.

SPAIN

Insert at least 150 Pesetas in sloping groove at top of payphone (do not press button to left of dial). Lift receiver, check for dial tone, dial. A signal indicates when to insert more money. Fully unused coins will be refunded. .
Coins accepted: 5, 25, 50, 100 Ptas (newer payphones also accept 200, 500, 1,000 Ptas). Phonecards: 1,000, 2,000, 5,000 Ptas (available from post offices, tobacconists and some banks). Local international operator: 008 Barcelona, Madrid; 9198 or 9398 elsewhere. UK Direct operator: 900 99 00 44. Reverse charge calls available. Cheap rate: Daily 2200-0800. BT Chargecard Direct number 900 99 0044.

SWEDEN

Lift receiver, check for dial tone. Insert at least 2 Kronor or phonecard, dial. A signal of two tones indicates when to insert more money. Fully unused coins refunded. Coins accepted: 50 Ore; 1, 5 Kr. Phonecards: 25, 50, 100 Kr. Local international operator: 0018. UK Direct operator: 020 795 144. Reverse charge calls available. BT Chargecard Direct number 020 795 144.

SWITZERLAND

Lift receiver, check for dial tone. Insert at least 40c or phonecard, dial. A signal indicates when to insert more money. Fully unused coins refunded.
Coins accepted: 10, 20, 50c; 1, 2, 5F. Phonecards: 10, 20F (available from post offices and newsagents). Local international operator: 114. UK Direct operator: 155 2444. Reverse charge calls available. Cheap rate: Mon-Fri 2100-0800, all weekend. BT Chargecard Direct number 155 2444.

TURKEY

Lift receiver, check for dial tone. Insert token or phonecard, dial. A signal indicates when to insert more tokens or phonecard. Fully unused tokens refunded.
Coins accepted: Tokens only, min.value 750TL (from post offices). Phonecards: 4,300, 8,600, 17,100TL (from post offices). Local international operator: 032 Ankara, Istanbul, Izmir; 062 other cities. UK Direct Operator: 00 800 44 11770. Reverse charge calls available. BT Chargecard Direct number 800 44 1177.

You can use millions of UK phones to make BT Chargecard calls, including all BT public payphones.

A BT Chargecard is available FREE on 0800 800 893

COMING HOME

CUSTOMS ALLOWANCES

	Duty Free Goods obtained anywhere outside the EU or duty and tax free within the EU, including purchases from a UK duty free shop	Duty Paid Goods obtained duty and tax paid in the EU
Cigarettes, or Cigarillos, or Cigars, or Tobacco	200 100 50 250g	800 400 200 1kg
Still table wine	2 litres	* see below
Spirits, strong liqueurs over 22% volume, or	1 litre	10 litres
Fortified or sparkling wines, other liqueurs	2 litres	* 20 litres of fortified wine, or 90 litres of wine (of which no more than 60 litres of sparkling wine)
Perfume	50g/60cc (2 fl oz)	no limit
Toilet water	250cc (9 fl oz)	no limit
All other goods including gifts and souvenirs	£71 worth, but no more than 50 litres of beer, 25 mechanical lighters	no limit except for the beer allowance, which is increased to 110 litres

Duty-free sales
The EU has reprieved duty-free sales until 1999. Under an agreed Community system for each journey to another member state of the EU, you are entitled to buy the quantities of duty-free goods shown above.

Duty-paid goods
Provided they are for your personal use, there is no further tax to be paid on goods you have obtained duty and tax paid in the European Union. Personal use includes gifts.
Member states still reserve the right to check that products are for personal use only, and not for resale purposes. For this reason, the EU has set guide levels, as shown above, and if you bring more than the amounts in the guide levels you are required to show that the goods are for your personal use.

Travelling within the EU
If you are travelling to the UK directly from another EU country, you do not need to go through a red or green channel, and you do not need to make any declaration to Customs. However, selective checks will still be carried out by Customs to detect prohibited goods.

ENTERING THE UK

You may have valuable items such as cameras, radios or watches which were bought in the UK, or which have been brought through Customs before and any Customs charges paid. It is a good idea to carry receipts for these items where possible, so that they can be checked by a Customs officer if necessary.

If you are entering the UK in a vehicle, it is important that everyone travelling with you knows what goods are prohibited or restricted. If goods are smuggled in a car, the car may be confiscated.

Never carry anything into the UK for someone else.

No-one under the age of 17 is entitled to tobacco or drink allowances.

PROHIBITED AND RESTRICTED GOODS

In order to protect health and the environment, certain goods cannot be freely imported. The main items are as follows:

Animals, birds and reptiles The importation of most species, whether alive or dead (eg stuffed), and many items derived from protected species, eg fur skins, ivory, reptile leather and goods made from them, is restricted. Such items can be imported only if you have prior authority (eg a licence) to import them.

Counterfeit or 'Copy' Goods Goods bearing a false indication of their origin and goods in breach of UK copyright are prohibited and must not be brought into the UK.

Drugs Do not import controlled drugs, eg heroin, cocaine, cannabis, amphetamines and LSD. If you require drugs for medical reasons, further information can be obtained from: The Home Office Drugs Branch, 50 Queen Anne's Gate, London SW1H 9AT.

Endangered Species The Department of the Environment operates controls on the import of endangered species. Enquiries should be made to: DoE, Endangered Species Branch, Tollgate House, Houlton Street, Bristol BS2 9DJ. ☎ 0117-921 8202

Firearms and Ammunition Firearms and ammunition (including gas pistols, gas canisters, electric shock batons and similar weapons) are restricted and can be imported only if you have prior authority (eg a licence) to import them. Explosives (including fireworks) are banned completely.

Foodstuffs The importation of meat, poultry and their products including ham, bacon, sausage, pâté, eggs, milk and cream is restricted.

Pets Cats, dogs and other mammals must not be brought into the UK unless a British import licence (rabies) has previously been issued. A period of six months quarantine is required. All live birds also require an import licence.

Plants There is currently an exception to the requirements for a health certificate for plants and plant produce imported as passenger baggage from any country within the European-Mediterranean area, provided the consignment does not exceed:

- up to 2 kg of tubers, bulbs and corms free of soil
- up to 5 plants or cuttings
- a small bouquet of cut flowers
- up to 2 kg of fruit and vegetables together (but not potatoes) – because of the danger of importing Colorado beetle)
- up to 5 retail packets of seeds

This concessional arrangement does not apply to: plants & seeds of the genus 'beta'; forest trees; fruit tree material (including Bonsai); Chrysanthemums; vine plants; cut Gladioli; Fodder Pea seeds; plants of the grass family (Graminae).

There are no restrictions on flower seeds from any country. Should you wish to import more than these quantities you will have to obtain a phytosanitary certificate from the Plant Protection Service in the country of origin.

Further details can be obtained from: Plant Health Division, Ministry of Agriculture, Fisheries and Food, Foss House, Kings Pool, York YO1 2PX. ☎ 01904 641000.

Other prohibited goods include offensive weapons such as flick knives, butterfly knives, knuckledusters, swordsticks, and some martial arts weapons; counterfeit currency; radio transmitters and cordless telephones not approved for use in the UK; obscene books, videos etc; horror comics; anglers' lead weights.